D1072090

A METHOD OF
INTERPRETING LITERATURE

This book contains three lectures delivered at Smith College in February, 1948, and constitutes the third of a series of volumes of Smith College lectures.

A Method of
INTERPRETING
LITERATURE

by

LEO SPITZER, Ph.D.

Professor of Romance Philology
The Johns Hopkins University

NEW YORK / RUSSELL & RUSSELL

All' amico Singleton,
per tanti anni compagno di studi e di armi, alla Hopkins,
per l'occasione della sua inaugurazione
all' olimpica vetta della cattedra italiana di Harvard

1.VII.1948

CONTENTS

Three Lectures Given

as the

Third Annual Smith College Lecture Series
February 5, 12 and 19, 1948

•

1. Three Poems on Ecstasy   1
   (John Donne, St. John of the Cross,
      Richard Wagner)

2. Pages from Voltaire   64

3. American Advertising Explained
      as Popular Art   102

A METHOD OF
INTERPRETING LITERATURE

THREE POEMS ON ECSTASY

(JOHN DONNE, ST. JOHN OF THE CROSS, RICHARD WAGNER)

IN AN ARTICLE entitled "A Farewell to Criticism," the American poet Karl Shapiro has written (*Poetry*, Jan. 1948):

> I question the principle underlying *explication de texte*. A poem should not be used as a subject for linguistic, semantic, or psychological study. . . . Poetry is not language, but a language *sui generis* which can be understood, paraphrased, or translated only as poetry. . . . The same word used in a line of prose and a line of poetry are really two different words, not even similar, except in appearance. I would designate the poetry word as "not-word" . . . a poem is a literary construct composed of not-words which, in their retreat from meanings, arrive at a prosodic sense-beyond-sense. The aim of a poem is not known. (By "prosody" Mr. Shapiro means not only poetic rhythm but also poetic associations and figures of speech.)

Accordingly, what I wish to attempt in this series of lectures (*explication de texte* applied to poetry) should, in the opinion of a poet of real authority, be resolutely eschewed. Now the literary critic who is

1

able to draw on his historical knowledge, may discount the periodically recurring revolt of poets against critics who would explain their poetry; this is a "poetic" attitude which dates from the period of Romanticism. It would not have occurred to a Dante, a St. John of the Cross, a Racine, a Milton, to doubt that their poetry, representative, or so they thought, of universal feelings, could be explained by their fellow-men; indeed, these poets often took pains, themselves, to explain their poetry. But, since the discovery, in the eighteenth century, of the "original genius" who is supposed to speak not for mankind, but for himself alone—since that time the irrational meaning of their poetry has been stressed by the poets more and more; we have all heard of such stock situations as, for example, that of the professor of French literature explaining the meaning of Valéry's *Cimetière Marin* in one of the *amphithéâtres* of the Sorbonne, while the author was sitting in the gallery, his gentle smile expressing a skeptical *que sais-je?* as he listened to the positive statements of the commentator. It is, of course, the prerogative, perhaps the duty, of the poet of today to defend the irrational, the somehow "aimless" nature of his creation against any unilateral, rational or behavioristic explanation. But there is also to be considered the undeniable fact that *language*, the particular medium of the poet, is itself a system both rational and irrational; it is lifted by him to a plane of still greater irrationalism while nevertheless maintaining its ties with the normal, mainly rational language. It is simply not true that poetry consists of "not-words" (except perhaps in the case of the *dadaistes*, or the recent sect of *lettristes*, who coin words non-existent in their own or in any human language). Poetry generally consists of words belonging to a given language which have irrational as well as rational connotations, words which become transfigured by what Shapiro calls "prosody." If we pause to consider a stanza from one of the poems of Mr. Shapiro himself, the poem *Nostalgia* (which can hardly be called "aimless" since an aim, that of portraying nostalgia, is stated in the title and is so understood by the reader), we shall see that he makes a constant appeal to the usual connotations, that is, to the prose (but not entirely prose) connotations of English words:

> My soul stands at the window of my room
> And I ten thousand miles away;
> My days are filled with Ocean's sound of doom,
> Salt and cloud and the bitter spray,
> Let the wind blow, for many a man shall die.

Not only is the outward and the inner situation clear (the world-war soldier Karl Shapiro, who fought in the Pacific, looking out from his window upon the Ocean and thinking of the fate of so many fellow-

soldiers who would not see their homeland again);
it is true also that the prosody is assimilable and ex-
plainable: the fifth line, which happens to be the
refrain of the whole poem, breaks the rhythm of the
preceding quatrain with its initial anapaest and the
subsequent shock of two tonic syllables ("let the
wínd blów"), thereby evoking the impact of the
doom already foreshadowed in the static sense, but
now emergent, actual: "for many a man shall die."
But in this refrain the words *wind* and *blow, man*
and *die* are still those of our language, which have
preserved their usual connotations (and these connotations are in themselves not entirely rational); it
is only by their arrangement in our causal sentence,
—or rather pseudocausal sentence, for there is no
necessary connection between the blowing of the
wind and the death of many a man—and by the
rhythm already described, that another plane is suggested, that of poetry. Thus, by means of words of
our daily life, there is given the possibility of a logic
beyond our human logic, the logic of the doom that
wills the blowing of the wind in order that men may
die. The experienced reader will immediately think
of the technique of the folk-ballad, of Villon's "Mais
où sont les neiges d'antan?" or of the song at the
end of *Twelfth Night:* "The rain it raineth every
day"—in which trivial-seeming sentences are given
a new function: that of suggesting the necessity of

submitting to fate as figured by the elements. Instead of saying that poetry consists of "not-words
which, in their retreat from meaning, arrive at a
prosodic sense-beyond-sense," I would offer the suggestion that it consists of *words*, with their meaning
preserved, which, through the magic of the poet
who works within a "prosodic" whole, arrive at a
sense-beyond-sense; and that it is the task of the
philologist to point out the manner in which the
transfiguration just mentioned has been achieved.
The irrationality of the poem need not lose anything
at the hands of a discreet linguistic critic; on the
contrary, he will work in accord with the poet (although with no regard to his approval), insofar as
he will patiently and analytically retrace the way
from the rational to the irrational: a distance which
the poet may have covered in one bold leap.

* * *

I shall take up three poems dealing with approxi-
mately the same subject matter (the ecstatic union
of a human ego with a non-ego), in order to study
the magic transformation which actual words of the
particular language have undergone at the hands of
the poets who have succeeded in making their inner experience a poetic reality for the reader.

John Donne's poem "The Extasie" (published in
1633) begins by describing the outward situation of

two lovers, reclining on a grassy, violet-scented
mound near a river bank; against this background
they experience mystic union of a Neo-Platonic order, without being diverted or disturbed by physical passion.[1]

Where, like a pillow on a bed,
   A pregnant banke swel'd up, to rest
The violets reclining head,
   Sat we two, one anothers best.
Our hands were firmely cimented   5
   With a fast balme, which thence did spring,
Our eye-beames twisted, and did thred
   Our eyes, upon one double string;
So to'entergraft our hands, as yet
   Was all the meanes to make us one,   10
And pictures in our eyes to get
   Was all our propagation.
As 'twixt two equall Armies, Fate
   Suspends uncertaine victorie,
Our soules, (which to advance their state,   15
   Were gone out,) hung 'twixt her, and mee.
And whil'st our soules negotiate there,
   Wee like sepulchrall statues lay;
All day, the same our postures were,
   And wee said nothing, all the day.   20
If any, so by love refin'd,
   That he soules language understood,
And by good love were growen all minde,
   Within convenient distance stood,
He (though he knew not which soule spake,   25
   Because both meant, both spake the same)

6

Might thence a new concoction take,
  And part farre purer then he came.
This Extasie doth unperplex
  (We said) and tell us what we love,   30
Wee see by this, it was not sexe,
  Wee see, we saw not what did move:
But as all severall soules containe
  Mixtures of things, they know not what,
Love, these mixt soules, doth mixe againe,   35
  And make both one, each this and that.
A single violet transplant,
  The strength, the colour, and the size,
(All which before was poore, and scant,)
  Redoubles still, and multiplies.   40
When love, with one another so
  Interinanimates two soules,
That abler soule, which thence doth flow,
  Defects of lonelinesse controules.
Wee then, who are this new soule, know,   45
  Of what we are compos'd, and made,
For, th' Atomies of which we grow,
  Are soules, whom no change can invade.
But O alas so long so farre
  Our bodies why doe wee forbeare?   50
They are ours, though they are not wee, Wee are
  The intelligences, they the spheare.
We owe them thankes, because they thus,
  Did us, to us, at first convay,
Yeelded their forces, sense, to us,   55
  Nor are drosse to us, but allay.
On man heavens influence workes not so,
  But that it first imprints the ayre,

Soe soule into the soule may flow,
  Though it to body first repaire.   60
As our blood labours to beget
  Spirits, as like soules as it can,
Because such fingers need to knit
  That subtile knot, which makes us man:
So must pure lovers soules descend   65
  T'affections, and to faculties,
Which sense may reach and apprehend,
  Else a great Prince in prison lies.
To'our bodies turne wee then, that so
  Weake men on love reveal'd may looke;   70
Loves mysteries in soules doe grow,
  But yet the body is his booke.
And if some lover, such as wee,
  Have heard this dialogue of one,
Let him still marke us, he shall see   75
  Small change, when we'are to bodies gone.

The author evidently intends to offer, in poetic
guise, an intellectual definition of the ecstatic state
of two souls, which emerge from their bodies and
blend so completely that they become one. The
Greek term *ekstasis,* "going forth," is literally para-
phrased in line 14: "Our soules, (which to advance
their state, were *gone out,*)," a line which must be
contrasted with the final one: "Small change, when
we'are *to bodies gone*"; *i.e.,* when we return to un-
ecstatic normal life. Two phenomena must be described by the poet: the separation of soul from
body (the *ekstasis* proper) and the union of the two

8

souls. Both are explained by a technique of insisting and re-insisting on the same facts which are described with a wealth of variations. I shall list first the varied references to the idea: "two become one":

4	we two one anothers best
5	our hands were firmely cimented
8	thred our eyes upon one double string
9–10	to entergraft our hands, . . . to make us one
15–16	our soules . . . hung 'twixt her and mee
26	both meant, both spake the same
35	(love these) mixt soules (doth mixe againe)
36	makes both one, each this and that
41–42	[love] with one another . . . interinanimates [= animates] two soules
59	soule into the soule may flow
74	this dialogue of one

The concept of "union" suggests the corollary idea of "procreation"; and, indeed in our poem, we shall find references to the fruit of the lovers' union —which must be on the same spiritual plane as the union itself:

5–6	[our hands were firmely cimented] with a fast balme, which *thence did spring*
11–12	[pictures . . . was all our] propagation
15	our soules, (which to *advance their state* were gone out)
27	[he who would be a witness to our union]

9

      thence a new concoction [= distillate, state
      of maturation] take
43   that *abler* soule, which thence doth flow
45   wee, then, who are *this new soule*

And we may add further the first two lines: "Where, like a pillow on a bed, / A Pregnant banke swel'd up," which give to the intellectual procreation of the lovers a background of exuberantly fertile nature and vegetative life;[2] this passage should be taken together with ll. 37-40 (though this quatrain may strike us as a later interpolation): just as a single violet, transplanted into new soil, thrives with renewed life, so the single souls, offered a new soil by love (the soil of two-ness), will "redouble and multiply" their potentialities.

As for the idea of the ecstasy proper, this is taken up in the simile (ll. 13-17) of the two armies between which Fate hangs and for which the souls negotiate—a simile which is carried over into the following image of a double tombstone with recumbent figures from which the souls have fled. Again the idea of the unembodied souls recurs in line 22 ("by good love . . . growen all minde") and in ll. 47-48: "For th'Atomies of which we grow, / Are soules, whom no change can invade"; "We [our soules] are / The intelligences, they [our bodies] the spheare" (in medieval cosmology the spheres are moved by the angelic intelligences).

The last third of the poem is entirely given over to a justification of the body: since this must be abandoned if the soul would know ecstasy, one might assume that the body is only a hindrance for the spirit. And yet Donne insists on rehabilitating the body, describing the service it renders the spirit. By means of the senses the body mediates between the affianced souls: the body is not "drosse," but "allay" (l. 56). Moreover, it produces the blood-spirits (*spiritelli, esprits vitaux*) which are closely knit to the soul and produce those sensuous images that lead toward the revelation of love: "Loves mysteries in soules doe grow, / But yet the body is his booke." Donne ends by repeating the motif of the changelessness of souls that have once united in ecstasy.

We cannot escape the impression that the poet proceeds in the whole poem in the manner of a believer who has, firmly established in his mind, a conception of which he wishes to convince his audience. Indeed, so conscious is he of the need to *convince* others that, not content with the audience of his readers, he would introduce (l. 21) into the poem itself, "within convenient distance" of the lovers, a witness, or a listener, able to understand the language of love, who would listen to the "dialogue of one" (l. 73). Such a one, he assures us, could not but testify both to the purity of the mystic act and to the lasting effect of ecstasy, even after the return of the ecstatic souls to the bodies.

As for his audience of readers, the technique the poet adopts in order to convince us, is a quantitative one: he must multiply his evidence in order to hammer home his conviction. With ever-new similes (*to ciment, to graft, balm, concoction, to string, violet*), or with new coinages (*entergraft, interinanimate*) he forges the idea "two become one," and with accumulation of similes (negotiators for armies, sepulchral figures, intelligences not spheres, alloy not dross, mystery not book) the idea of ecstasy is given form. This revelation itself is portrayed from an intellectual point of view, as the paradoxical mathematical reduction: "2 becomes 1." The depth of the mystic experience, the feeling of its ever-increasing depth, is not expressed: nothing is revealed of the genesis of this experience, of the development up to the culminating moment of trance. The ecstasy has existed from the beginning: it is clearly named "this Extasie" in line 29: it lasts not a moment, but the whole day through. We are allowed to share only the enduring state of bliss-without-desire. Statuesque calm prevails throughout the poem. We see before us an allegorical statue of Ecstasis which stands unveiled from the beginning, while the flexible figures of speech circle about it, weaving ethereal wreaths around it, casting ever-new shadows

12

upon it—a composite allegorical figure indeed, of which are predicated attributes belonging to different realms of life. To express the same observation by varying the well-known couplet of Robert Frost:

They all dance around in a circle and suppose,
But the *concept* sits in the middle, and knows.

All the sciences and crafts are allowed to enter our poem in the form of metaphors and to testify to the central concept: the craft of the perfumer, of the jeweller who strings pearls, of the gardener who transplants, of the military negotiator, of the sculptor, of the alchemist who distills "concoctions," of the cosmologist who deals with the atomic structure of the universe—they all parade before the statue in a pageant, a Petrarchian *triumphus pudicitiae*.

Connected with Donne's quantitative procedure is his use of hyperbole, often misunderstood by the critics: he tells us that so great was the ecstasy, that (ll. 7-8) "Our eye-beames twisted, and did thred / Our eyes, upon one double string"—a feat none too easily visualized. But he means, of course, to predicate the impossible. According to the requirements of metaphysical wit, he must ascribe to what he praises the physically impossible as well as the limitless: not only must he marshal all the kaleidoscopic richness of the earth, he must introduce the unvisualizable possibilities of the impossible—well

13

aware that with all his effort his panegyric must, in the end, still be an approximation. Of course, this type of eulogy has the effect of distancing the object of praise: Donne does not re-enact what is within him, but points us to something above him. Instead of the re-creation of the intuitive experience the poet actually had, with its particular quality, we are offered an encyclopedic, discursive analysis. Yet this is informed by rhythmic beauty: the beauty of the rhythm of simple spoken speech with all its convincingness—a rhythm that echoes the inner event and testifies to the veracity of the report. Notice the rhythm (indicating "sameness" by chiastic "return to the same"), which accompanies the simile of the "sepulchre" (ll. 18-20):

> We like sepulchrall statues lay;
> *All day*, the same our postures were,
> And wee said nothing, *all the day*.

The rhythm by which the "new soul" is portrayed as beyond change (ll. 45-48):

> Wee, then, who are this new soule, know,
> Of what we are compos'd, and made,
> For, th'Atomies of which we grow,
> Are soules, *whom no change can invade*.

or the meditative rhythm of the lines that indicate the non-sexual nature of that love (ll. 31-32):

> *Wee see* by this, it was not sexe,
> *Wee see, we saw* not what did move. . . .

14

It can be no chance that the rhythm chosen by the poet is most convincing where the immutability of the union is contrasted with transient phenomena.

After having noted that in our poem the intellectual kernel of an intuitive state of mind has been made concrete and that an experience which must have developed in time has been reduced to timelessness, we may observe that the last part, that in which the justification of the body is offered (love begins in the body and will continue when the souls have returned to the body), is poetically less successful than the rest—and this, in spite of occasional poetic gems, such as (l. 64) "That subtile knot, which makes us man" (a line which turns the succinct definition of the psycho-physical nature of man into poetry), or (l. 68) "Else a great Prince in prison lies," where for one moment we seem to see the Segismundo of Calderon in his tower, deprived of the light of his senses. The final part of the poem verges on a scientific treatise of physiology, that is, of seventeenth-century physiology. Any reader must feel here a poetic anti-climax (he may even suspect composition of that last part at a different time): after we have known of the ecstasy of two souls become one, the idea of their return or "descent" to that body is disconcerting. For mortal man is so constituted that he can visualize a state of bliss only as an apex that must stand out in isolation, a death within life followed by silence; Goethe's Egmont exclaims: "Let me die, the world has no joy greater than this," and the curtain must fall. Donne, however, wished to make the ecstatic vision tributary to the daily life which must follow—and which could be enhanced by the remembrance thereof. But this very noble moral thought, so deeply connected with religious reformation and regeneration, has not come to poetic fruition; for, after having shared an ecstasy which is beyond time and change, we are not ready to return to the world where change, however slight, is possible. And the repetition of the motif of the witness who would observe the lovers in their post-ecstatic life is an indication that here Donne's poetic imagination was lagging.

Moreover, we feel somehow that Donne himself, in spite of his endeavor to justify the flesh, was more intimately convinced of the reality and beauty of the spiritual union than of the necessity of the body for that union. It may well be that the basically Protestant mind of Donne is responsible for this self-contradictory attitude. For estrangement from the body may be said to be characteristic of Protestantism, whereas in the Jewish faith the rights of the body can easily coexist with the claims of the Creator on man's immortal soul, and, in the Catholic religion, a bridge from soul to body is afforded by the church sacrament according to which Christ is present in the bodily union of the believers, who are *membra Christi*. In the Protestant monument erected by Donne to the mystic union, the figures impersonating this union show the touch of a firmer hand than does the pedestal of clay by which he would have them supported. Donne knows, in fact, no true answer to that tormenting question: "But O alas, so long, so farre / Our bodies why doe wee forbeare?" It is no chance that the word *sex* (l. 31) is used in our poem for the first time in European literature in the modern sense of the specific, objective, definable, but questionable, urge that conditions the life of man and woman.[3] Again in his poem *The Primrose* Donne says: ". . . should she / Be more then woman, shee would get above / All thought of sexe . . ."; to "get above all thought of sexe" goes hand in hand with "Wee see by this, it was not sexe": in both cases, "sex" is treated as a lesser factor which exists to be transcended.

However, if sex is envisaged (so sharply!) as a thing to be dismissed, we can, of course, not expect to find in Donne a representative of religious mysticism, which (as we know from Evelyn Underhill's studies on mystical psychology) borrows from sex the raw material of psycho-physical sensitivity with which to welcome, on a higher plane, *but still in one's body* as well as in one's soul, the invasion of the divine.

17

It is the Spanish mystics who, in their procedure of giving flesh to spiritual experience (while sharing Donne's ultimate attitude of disillusion, *desengaño,* toward the body), have found the most direct way to reconcile the splendor of the body, re-discovered by the Renaissance, and the supernatural beauty of divine grace, experienced in medieval meditation. And yet, our poem, with its clear demarcation between body and soul, will remain a monument of intellectual clarity. How characteristic is the verb *unperplex* (l. 29) which Donne has coined (and allowed to rhyme with *sex*—a counterbalance!), how revelatory of Donne's passionate desire for intellectual clarification of emotions! And it is this urge which has made John Donne so dear to our age, an age sore perplexed, mistrusting instinctual emotion—preferring, perhaps, clarity of analysis to syntheses which it can no longer wholeheartedly ratify.

※　※　※

In view of the interpretation I have just suggested for Donne's poem, it is hardly necessary to state that I am utterly opposed to the opinion offered by the late Professor Legouis in his *Histoire de la littérature anglaise.* Legouis, who evidently has in mind the numerous poems in which Donne has ridiculed the theme of Platonic love (think of *The Flea!*), sees in our poem a "sophistical" and "insidious" plea for physical consummation. The two lovers, after hav-

18

ing enjoyed for a full day the sensation of having formed one soul,

> sentent qu'ils sont devenus de purs esprits. De la hauteur où ils planent, que le corps est peu de chose! Pauvre corps, mais qui pourtant mérite sa récompense pour les avoir menés l'un vers l'autre. Il n'est que juste de penser à lui! "Pourquoi s'abstiennent nos corps si longtemps? . . . Sans cela un grand prince gît en prison."

Now, in order to justify such a carnal interpretation, Legouis has interpreted line 50 ("Our bodies why doe wee forbeare?") as if *forbear* meant, not "endure, tolerate," as I have understood it, but "restrain, control" ("pourquoi s'abstiennent nos corps si longtemps?"). Furthermore, in the last line: "Small change, when we'are to bodies gone," which I have explained as referring to the inevitable return from ecstasy to every-day life, he evidently sees an allusion to physical love. And what we have taken as a description of the beginning of love (which must start with the body), as a point from which to reach the ecstasy—he assumes to constitute an invitation, *hic et nunc,* to indulge the body; and the noble line 68: "Else a great Prince in prison lies," descriptive of the mortal condition of man, he brings in, somehow, as the climax of the carnal invitation: the individual man's eternal self-pitying plea to the woman.

Before such Gallic worldly wisdom, such familiarity with the age-old stratagems of a resourceful seducer (of a Valmont in the *Liaisons Dangereuses*), how naïve my own earnest remarks may appear! It sometimes happens, however, that candor is the most direct way of understanding; I have chosen simply to believe the poet when he speaks, at the beginning, with the unmistakable voice of truth, of the beauty, and reality, of the spiritual ekstasis: and if we do believe him here, we can not, then, see in the last part an invitation to carnality—which could only mean that the first part was a mere stratagem. And the lines with their sincere and final ring, "Wee see by this, it was not sexe, / Wee see, we saw not what did move"—is this the tone of hypocrisy? We should suspect that the speaker knew at the time that sex *did* move (or would move)? And that witness upon whom Donne calls at the end, "When we'are to bodies gone"—incredible to think that Donne is calling upon him to witness the physical act: he whom the poet has described as "by good love . . . growen all minde" (notice the lofty Augustinian phrase *good love = amor bonus*)!

No, I still prefer to see in our poem a glorification of true ekstasis (lacking perhaps in artistic convincingness, for the noble reason earlier suggested) rather than a circuitous exhibition of lofty Neo-Platonic philosophy destined only to bring about the inevitable earthy dénouement: I see in it, not an

argumentum ad hominem, or rather . . . *ad feminam,*
but, in accord with Donne himself, a "dialogue of
one"—of, if you wish, a monologue of two.

※　　※　　※

We have said that the Jewish sensibility—and I
believe this to be as true today as in the days of the
patriarchs—admits the coexistence of the body and
the soul in the presence of God, but with no attempt
at fusing them. It is then not surprising that a sensuous Oriental epithalamium that had found access
to the Jewish biblical canon, the *Song of Songs* (that
"herrlichste Sammlung Liebeslieder, die *Gott ge-
schaffen hat"*, as Goethe called it), should have
been, by Christian exegesis, transformed into an
allegorical treatise of mystic union. And it is this
mystical theme that we find in the Spanish poem
En una noche escura—which might be described as
a Catholic *Song of Songs* (for, indeed, it derives its
inspiration from the re-interpreted Hebrew canticle).
This poem, written about 1577 by the Carmelite
monk San Juan de la Cruz, is a perfect example of
the manner in which the body can be made artisti-
cally tributary to the mystic experience. The Catholic saint treats no lesser subject than the ecstatic
union, not with a human being, but with the divine,
in terms that constantly fuse soul and body:

　1.　En una noche escura,

21

Con ansias en amores inflamada,
¡Oh dichosa ventura!
Salí sin ser notada,
Estando ya mi casa sosegada;

2. A escuras y segura,
Por la secreta escala, disfrazada,
¡Oh dichosa ventura!
A escuras, y en celada,
Estando ya mi casa sosegada.

3. En la noche dichosa,
En secreto, que nadie me veía,
Ni yo miraba cosa,
Sin otra luz y guía,
Sino la que en el corazon ardía,

4. Aquesta me guiaba
Más cierto que la luz del mediodía,
Adonde me esperaba
Quien yo bien me sabía
En parte donde nadie parecía.

5. ¡Oh noche, que guiaste,
Oh noche amable más que la alborada,
Oh noche, que juntaste
Amado con amada,
Amada en el Amado transformada!

6. En mi pecho.florido,
Que entero para él solo so guardaba,
Allí quedó dormido,
Y yo le regalaba,
Y el ventalle de cedros aire daba.

7. El aire del almena,
    Cuando yo sus cabellos esparcía,
    Con su mano serena
    En mi cuello hería
    Y todos mis sentidos suspendía.

8. Quedéme y olvidéme,
    El rostro recliné sobre el Amado;
    Cesó todo, y dejéme,
    Dejando mi cuidado
    Entre las azucenas olvidado.

This poem, as has been recognized by its finest commentators, the Frenchman Baruzi[4] and the Spaniard Dámaso Alonso,[5] falls into three parts: the beginning of the soul's pilgrimage, stanza 1-4; the arrival and the announcement of the mystic union, stanza 5; and the scene of the union itself, stanza 5-8. In order to gain insight into the poetic organism, let us begin again by a "list," as we have done before in the explanation of Donne's poem! There it was the sequence of similes that allowed us to penetrate into the poet's procedure of composition; here, however, we shall start with an (at first glance) trivial linguistic detail: starting from the point of view of tense usage, let us draw up a list of the preterites used in our short narrative, because it is by these that the action is carried forward: they form, as it were, the dramatic framework, expressing an unbroken development. We shall see them increase at the end of the poem: in Part I there is only *salí,* "I started forth" (stanza 1); in Part II (stanza 5) only *guiaste,* "you [the night] led me," and *juntaste,* "you joined us"; in Part III, in addition to *allí quedó dormido,* "my love fell asleep," of stanza 6, we find five preterites in the last stanza, four of them verbs of bodily movement; the action, as I said, is conceived in bodily terms. This climactic increase in dramatic tenses toward the end coincides, strangely enough, with a decrease in voluntary or dynamic action on the part of the protagonist: the loving soul that in Part I started forth resolutely on its pilgrimage, is, in Part II, led forward by the night, and it is the night that joins the soul with its Beloved (who is himself passive: *quedó dormido*)—whereupon all striving ceases; and the activity of the soul in the last stanza is one of gradual self-extinction: *cesó todo.* This contrast between the accumulation of dramatic tenses and the *smorzando* of the activities they express, is paradoxical:[6] the climax of action is reached in non-action, in the receiving of the mystic invasion (which can be only a gift of divine grace), in self-annihilation. The first preterite *salí* was an élan motivated "con ansias en amores inflamada," by the burning anxiety of the flame of love; the *dejéme* of the end, though expressing self-abandonment, melts immediately into "dejando mi cuidado . . . olvidado" ("leaving my sorrow forgot-

24

ten"): the cessation of all perturbation. The action
of the Spanish poem which begins with a movement
dictated by pain and by the will to still pain, ends
with the achievement of self-forgetfulness free from
pain.

After having gained a bird's-eye view of the
whole and of the salient features of its structure,
let us now return to the beginning and seek to analyze in their turn the three parts we have isolated.

In the first stanza, as has already been said, the
outstanding word which starts the movement of the
poem is *salí*. But we may ask ourselves: who is it
that started forth? Who is the protagonist of the
poem? The participle *inflamada* (stanza 1), followed by *notada* and later by *amada* and *transformada* (stanza 5), would seem to indicate a feminine being; and since this being speaks of joining
her Beloved (*Amado*), we might be justified in seeing the action in terms of an earthly love. Or is this
feminine aspect predicated only of that spiritual being, the soul (Spanish *alma*, a word never mentioned
in our poem), eternally conceived as feminine? This
ambiguity is obviously intended by the author not
only because of his desire to express figuratively the
spiritual by the physical: it is true also that, just
because the identity of the protagonist is presented
as self-evident, as needing no elucidation, we are
drawn immediately into the atmosphere of the one

who speaks of her love, and we can share, unquestioningly, in her experience, as this develops in the poem.

To return again to *salí:* whence was this departure? From what background does this sudden movement emerge? But it is only the first two stanzas *taken together* that give us this background; indeed, these two stanzas must, as Dámaso Alonso has pointed out, be taken as one sentence (not to be separated by a period, as is done in all the editions): they contain the same rhymes, and, if considered as a unit, the opening period will show that *parellelismus membrorum* characteristic of the Hebrew model (the *Song of Songs*): compare the parallelisms in

> By night on my bed I sought him whom my soul
> loveth
> I sought him, but I found him not.
> I said, I will rise now, and go about the city,
> In the streets and in the broad ways,
> I will seek him whom my soul loveth.
> I sought him, but I found him not.

and in our poem:

> En una noche escura,
> Con ansias en amores inflamada,
> ¡Oh dichosa ventura!
> Salí sin ser notada,
> Estando ya mi casa sosegada;

A escuras y segura,
Por la secreta escala, disfrazada,
¡Oh dichosa ventura!
A escuras, y en celada,
Estando ya mi casa sosegada.

These musical, even dance-like cadences help situate our poem in the climate of Biblical mystery, in which movements that would seem erratic to the uninitiated, are guided by Providence. In the stillness of the night we hear those mysterious accents, supported, as it were, by *word-motifs* which repeat themselves with a consistency suggestive of continuity of will and purpose. Here the repetitions are not destined to bring one concept to full clarity by ever-new similes, as were those of Donne; instead, we find a few very simple word-motifs parsimoniously repeated with only slight variation: indeed "¡Oh dichosa ventura!" is repeated without change, as is also *estando ya mi casa sosegada:* these establish the homology of the two stanzas. Again in the sequence *en una noche escura—a escuras y segura—a escuras y en celada* we find one word (*escuro*) thrice repeated—while in the sequence *sin ser notada —secreta escala disfrazada—en celada* we have only thematic affinity, but still affinity. Not that there is always a musical *echo:* gentle contrasts may be heard: it is a soul stirred by passion that leaves the house now wrapped in silence (*inflamada—sose-*

27

gada); the darkness of the night (*a escuras*) is in op-
position to the sureness of the purpose (*segura*). And
the rhyming of *ventura* with *segura* also suggests a
contradiction—though this is softened by the fact
that the adventure is called *dichosa* ("blessed"). The
decision of the soul is, indeed, a *venture* into the unknown, an *adventure*, not in the trivial sense of today (a capricious interruption of everyday life), but
in the sense in which it has been said that in the
Middle Ages all of life was an adventure: man's
venturesome quest for the *advent* of the divine. The
soul that has here decided to meet the divine has
engaged itself in an existential adventure, and we
are assured of a response from the divine by the
epithet *dichosa*. And the word *escala*, with its suggestion of height, is the symbol of the upward development of the soul (we may remember the mystic
ladder of Bernard de Clairvaux).

The next two stanzas (which I would translate
as follows: "In the happy night, in secrecy—for no
one saw me nor saw I aught but the light of my
heart—, this light, brighter than the noon-day sun,
did guide me to the one whom I knew to be in a
place accessible to none other") should also be taken
together (though this suggestion has not been made
by others) because of the same rhymes in *-ia* and
also because of a discreet paralllism which runs
through them. Here we find again the alternation of

motifs which assures the continuous flow of the poem: the words *dichosa* and *secreta* of stanza 2 reappear; *sin ser notada* of stanza 2 is continued by *nadie me veía*, and *en celada* by *en parte donde nadie parecía.* We may also note that in this pair of stanzas the one main verb is the imperfect *guiaba.* Once the decision is made, announced dramatically by the preterite *salí*, the action may subside to a calm, steady, prolonged rhythm, suggestive of firm direction. And we sense a new note of serenity and clarity: *en una noche escura* has given way to *en la noche dichosa;* night has now become a familiar medium in which the soul knows its way. In this darkness a light appears which shines from the heart; and this light is first introduced negatively (*"without* a light . . . save that . . ."), as if, thereby, made to emerge out of darkness. It is this radiance by which the soul is guided (*guía–guiaba*) more surely than by the brightness of noon-day. And with the first line of stanza 4 there is suggested an outburst of glad relief: *aquesta me guiaba*, "this, this was my guide." Out of the maze of the third stanza, which suggests the movement of the soul as it feels its way through the darkness, there emerges, like a clearing, the sure guide; the wondrous light, which was first suggested tentatively (negatively as we have said) in a dependent clause, is now, in the main clause, hailed openly: *aquesta.* . . . The sentence structure is thus allowed to translate the consistent progress of the soul that has striven, encouraged by an inner hope (*segura–dichosa*), until now the light within her shines around her, beyond her, toward the goal, now well discerned (*adonde*), toward that one (*quien*) whose dwelling place is instinctively known to her ("one whom I knew to be in a place accessible to none other"). Here we have the idea of secret, exclusive knowledge, just as earlier there were suggestions of a secret, clandestine journey (the mystic ladder was "camouflaged," *disfrazada*). This motif of surreptitious love may be ultimately a remnant of the social-poetic conventions of the Troubadour love-poetry,[6a] but it has acquired with Juan de la Cruz a mystical sense; since Christian mysticism represents the highest development of the Christian belief in a personal God, Who conditions the immortal soul of man, as this, in turn, presupposes God—the *mystic* soul, then, is able to affirm its knowledge of that individual God, as it were, as its *personal* possession in isolation, even in secrecy. With these last lines the pilgrimage has come to an end: with the allusion to *quien* "one who" (that ambiguous pronoun which posits an individual without revealing his identity). Later, this beloved individual here alluded to by *quien* will appear as *amado* (line 4, st. 5) and finally as *el Amado* (in the following line).

30

We have been led, by the technique of musical variation and of a gradual syntactical unfolding, from the *noche escura* to the light that is brighter than day, from loneliness to the meeting with Him who is the divine goal—from what the Greeks would call στέρησις ("privation") to ἕξις ("possession"). These are basically terms of logic and indeed we find the idea of privation, of absence of positive characteristics, rendered by such negative grammatical elements as *sin, nadie, ni . . . cosa, sin, nadie,* which lead to the positive *aquesta* and *quien,* to fulfilment: "seeing nothing" leads to seeing the Beloved. Mysticism, indeed, posits privation, renunciation and purgation, as the starting-point toward fulfilment: expanding the Christian tenet that to have-not is ultimately to have, that only by closing one's eyes to the outward world does one truly see (the eyes of the heart, *oculi cordis,* are keener than the eyes of the senses), and that the light of the heart shines brighter than any other light.[6b]

And now we understand the jubilant exclamations with which the next part (consisting of one stanza alone) begins:

> ¡Oh noche, que guiaste,
> Oh noche amable más que la alborada,
> Oh noche, que juntaste . . . !

Here, too, there is a paradox: "night that didst guide." It is more natural to think of the light that

31

guides: but, then, as we know, the night has become light (στέρησις appears in the splendor of ἕξις). And this radiant night has also "joined together" (*juntaste*). This *juntaste* is the climax of the sequence *guiaba—guiaste—juntaste;* we have already noted that in *aquesta me guiaba* there was a new note of tranquillity (the momentum of will-power, originally announced by *salí*, has subsided, as the soul yields to the inner light); now with *¡oh noche que juntaste!* the guidance has become a successfully accomplished fact, and the initiative passes from the light of the heart to the *night* itself; and it is the night alone which brings about the union. This poetic symbol of the night, as the mediator of the spiritual marriage, is original with Juan de la Cruz, as Baruzi has pointed out—who would also distinguish between the *symbol* of the night as it is used in our poem, and the *allegory* of the night as we find this elaborated in the prose commentaries of our author.[7] For whereas allegory consists of an intellectual play wherein a series of fixed qualities belonging to one realm are made to correspond to a series of fixed qualities belonging to another realm (so that a literal "translation" is possible at any stage), a symbol represents an emotional identification of a complex of feelings with one outward object which, once the initial identification has been achieved, produces itself ever-new images, with their own rhythm and their own development, not always translatable. The symbol continually unfolds before us in time, while the allegory once developed, is fixed forever, as is the relationship of its details. The allegory of love in the *Roman de la Rose* can be translated step by step; for example, the rose is characterized by thorns, by a delightful odor, *etc.*, the allegorical implications of all of which are obvious. But the cross of Christ is a symbol: once Christ's suffering has been symbolized by that particular wooden instrument of torture, once Christ has "taken the cross on Himself," this Cross may become, in time, the "balance" on whose scales the sins of the world are weighed, the "tree" of life that conquers death, the "lyre" of Orpheus, etc. And with Juan de la Cruz the night is a similarly untranslatable symbol, generative of new situations and emotions which must be grasped as they unfold in time: it was first only the medium in which the lonely soul started its venturesome journey; now it has become the guide and (here no "translation" is actually possible) even the mediator between the Lover and the Beloved. Indeed the night itself is drawn into the atmosphere of *amar: noche amable.* Perhaps there is suggested an equation between night and love; surely it is love which joins the lovers, and yet it has been said of the night: *¡oh noche que juntaste. . . !* Therefore night = love. And, together with *amado* and *amada*, our

33

noche amable forms a triangle (implying the triune relationship).[8] The three variations of the stem *amar* are symbolical of this mystic alchemy.[9]

The *noche amable* which figures as the basic essence of the union, of the transformation of the *amada* into the *amado,* is actually referred to in line 2 of stanza 5 as *amable más que la alborada,* "more lovely than the dawn." Here we may see a continuation of the motif (st. 4), *más cierto que la luz del mediodía* (night more precious than day), in which the normal evaluation of night and day is reversed. The praise of the night at the expense of the day is also quite contrary to the tendency in the Christian hymns, of hailing the morning star or the crowing of the cock as signs of the defeat of the powers of darkness and evil by those of good. Nor, obviously, is our apostrophe: *¡oh noche amable más que la alborada!* to be compared to the *o vere beata nox!* of the Holy Saturday liturgy, which prepares the believer for the more important, the all-important resurrection of the Lord, which will take place on Easter Sunday. Perhaps the poetic inspiration may be traced here not only to the general tradition of Christian mysticism (v. note 6C), but also (again) to the Troubadour genre called the *alba,* in which so often the glory of the night, the night of love, is extolled to the disparagement of dawn.[10] Of course, the dramatic situation is not the same:

there is no friendly guard posted on the tower to warn the lovers (often in vain) of the danger of approaching dawn—for here no danger need be feared by the lovers.

And here it should be remarked that the mystical metamorphosis as described by Juan de la Cruz (*amada* becoming one with *el Amado*) implies no complementary transformation (*Amado* > *amada*); that is, no equality between the lovers, as was the case with Donne. The love described by Donne, even on a spiritual plane, is still the love which could never invite a metaphorical interpretation of union with the divine, because of his (very modern) concept of basic equality between the two lovers. If our Catholic poet is able to use human love as a figuration of love for the divine, this is because human love itself, according to age-old tradition, implies no equality: the bride submits to the bridegroom.

We have treated stanza 5 as representing the lyrical culmination of the poem, an interpretation borne out linguistically by the sequence of three apostrophes to the night. This exclamatory style has already been foreshadowed by the repetition of *¡oh dichosa ventura!*, parenthetically inserted. But now the exultant note comes to full *épanouissement* —and is expressed in a pattern which, in Judeo-Christian liturgy (it is not to be found in pagan lit-

urgy, according to Eduard Norden), was reserved
for addressing the deity: a vocative, followed by
relative clauses describing the triumphs or the favors of God, and usually followed in turn by a re-
quest for further favors[11] (though, in our poem, no
additional divine favor can be desired; the soul
wishes only to pour forth its gratefulness to the
charismatic power of love).

And now the scene of the *unio mystica:* with the
first lines of stanza 6, we sense immediately a new
stillness and composure—after the exultant, ringing
notes of the preceding stanza. Let us note first the
word *pecho* ("breast")—a word capable of both a
moral meaning (here, perhaps, "the heart") and, of
course, a physical meaning.[12] It is surely in the moral
sense that we must understand line 2: *que entero
para él solo se guardaba* ("which kept itself entire
for Him alone"), a line which makes explicit for the
first time the motivation, the monogamic motivation,
of the pilgrimage: of that *salí* which may have first
appeared prompted by sudden passion, but is now
revealed as springing from deep-set faithfulness to
the divine. And yet with *pecho florido* of the first
line, which means, no doubt, "flower-scented
breast," a suggestion of the sensuous is inescapable;
here the disembodied soul whose progress we have
followed acquires a mystical body. The preposi-
tional phrase *en mi pecho florido* may remind us of

the similar phrases *en una noche oscura* and *en la noche dichosa:* the framework of the background of the dark night gives way to that flower-scented breast on which the Beloved reposes: *En mi pecho florido . . . Allí quedó dormido.*

But in this *allí* ("on my breast, *there* he rested"), in this logically superfluous, somehow idiomatic adverb, do we not feel an emotional insistence ("there, in this place") as if on the breast as a goal attained— by the Beloved? So far, we have treated the pilgrimage only as a striving of the soul toward her own goal. And in describing her expectation we have, perhaps, passed over too easily the reference, in stanza 4, to the Bridegroom who was waiting (*esperaba*), waiting at the trysting-place. By now, in this one word *allí* we may catch the delicate suggestion of the quiet, steadfast yearning of the divine for the human soul[13]—whose relief from longing is now declared in the gently climactic *allí* (surely an echo of that *aquesta*, that sigh of relief with which the Bride greeted the guiding light).

There the divine sleeps. And it is while he sleeps that the soul knows its final mystic rapture (described only in the last stanza). This sleep of Christ, how is it to be understood? (The critics, all of them silent on this point, must have thought only of the Bridegroom of the *Song of Songs*, who is shown "as a bundle of myrrh, that lieth betwixt my breasts";

but it is not said there that he is sleeping.) The only suggestion that seems satisfactory to me is the hallowed medieval legend of the Unicorn, who, as the symbol of Christ, falls to sleep on the sweet-smelling breast of a virgin. Against this background, the *pecho florido* "that kept itself entire for Him alone" acquires a particular significance. And, in the idyllic scene centered about the quiescent divine, all activity is subdued, all the participants are hushed: divinity, the human soul, and Nature—the latter figured by the cedar trees (suggesting a Biblical landscape) gently fanned by the air. The idyllic quality of the scene is enhanced by the repetition of *and* which suggests never-ending tenderness: (*y yo le regalaba / y el ventalle de cedros aire daba*). The word *aire* is repeated in the first line of the next stanza; we seem still to be in the same gentle atmosphere lulled by a soft breeze—which perhaps plays with the hair of the Beloved as the Bride spreads it to the air. But let us not be deceived; it is *el aire del almena,* the air from the battlement (*almena,* the Spanish word of Arabic origin, implies a medieval castle and its tower). Does this not suggest warfare, sudden attack, hostile arrows? Dámaso Alonso has not sensed this military note: to him the tower is a place of pleasant refuge to which the lovers have ascended, to enjoy, according to him, the air gently blowing between the turrets.[14] But between these

two contradictory pictures evoked by two inter-
preters let common sense decide: are even the
cedars of Lebanon tall enough to reach up to the
turrets? And the lilies of the last stanza—would they
be growing on the tower? No, surely the lovers are
at the *foot* of the tower (among the lilies), beneath
the cedar trees.

And from this turreted tower, something strikes
and wounds (*hería*); it must be, though this has been
suggested by no other critic, *the arrow of love*, the
arrow by which Saint Teresa was pierced, in the
scene made graphically familiar to us by the statue
of Bernini. Our scene, of course, is not to be visualized so concretely, so plastically, or with such har-
rowing effect; the arrow that strikes the unprotected
neck is still only the air, and it strikes gently *con su
mano serena*—but it finds its mark and leaves sweet
death in its wake. This is the moment of ecstasy and
annihilation (*todos mis sentidos suspendía*), the familiar "theopathic" state experienced by all mystics
and often described by them as a blend of heavenly
sweetness and piercing pain.[15] And the gentle hand
that wounds suggests a bold personification which
does not, however, quite materialize: the *aire del
almena* does not harden into a figure of definable
contours (least of all into the figure of the gay archer
Cupid of Bernini): it remains in the state of that
vaporoso atmosphere of a Murillo. It is an intangi-

ble, an immaterial agent which, by an imperceptible activity, produces the climactic effect—while Christ sleeps. Is this air that wounds with serenity a symbol of the Holy Ghost, who is often compared, in Juan de la Cruz' commentaries, with air (cf. the relationship of Latin *spiritus* with *spirare,* "to breathe")? Perhaps we can not hope to penetrate the veil of mystery with which the Spanish Saint has wished to conceal as well as to reveal the mystery of the inactive activity, the Nature-like activity of the deity.

And now the last stanza, which may be said to render acoustically the gradual extinction of life: a love-death. Even before we come to this stanza we have learned that all the senses are suspended—as ours too must be: the sensations which had been earlier aroused (the olfactory sense [the flowers], the sense of touch [the air]) by now are numbed; the life of the senses, which came to its highest intensity in the mystic union, recedes; these have been stimulated by the poet only to make us realize the *spiritual* eroticism experienced by the mystic soul that will *abandon* the life of the senses. And this condition of deprivation or στέρησις is very aptly symbolized by the immaculately white lilies (*azucenas*), delicately profiled against the dawn, which lack a positive color (unlike the pomegranate of the love-scene in the *Song of Songs);* the Umbrian mystic Jacopone da Todi says of the mystic soul engulfed in the sea of

40

God: *en ben sí va notando / belleza contemplando la qual non ha colore,* "all its feeling swims in sweetness: it contemplates a beauty which has no color."[16] The suggestion of beatific nothingness, of gradual Lethean self-forgetfulness is achieved in our poem by a combination of two devices: we are offered a picture of bodily relaxation, leading to psychic extinction (*recliné mi rostro, dejéme*), together with an acoustic effect of lulling incantation, produced by the monotonous repetitions of sounds. As for the first, *el rostro recliné,* "I let my face fall," suggests clearly the physical; *dejéme,* "I abandoned myself," perhaps a blend of the physical and the spiritual; while, of course, *dejando mi cuidado,* "leaving my sorrow forgotten . . .," describes purely a state of the soul. The psycho-physical and the active-inactive aspect of the mystic experience could not be better expressed than by this ambivalent *dejar.* As for the acoustic devices, we may note the two variations on the verb *dejar (dejéme—dejando)* and the two on *olvidar,* "to forget" (*olvidéme—olvidado*), and particularly the repetition of the rhyme in -*éme* (*quedéme—olvidéme—dejéme*), which suggests a gradual sinking into the abyss of forgetfulness. And in the words *dejéme, / Dejando mi cuidado / Entre las azucenas olvidado,* which offer a final, lingering cadence, we have a transition from the act of abandoning the world to the state re-

41

sulting from this act: oblivion attained. In the final word *olvidado*, "already forgotten," this state is presented as an accomplished fact which must have taken place, somehow, before—so that when we actually come to the word *olvidado*, we know we have left it behind. The soul *is* already resolved in God. And this "already," the temporal adverb that I see implied in *dejando*, is the counterpart to the explicit *ya*, "already," of the first stanzas (*estando ya mi casa sosegada*): from the beginning to the end of the poem we are reminded of the progress in time of the mystic experience.

Juan de la Cruz has been able to transcribe the unbroken line, the parabola of that experience in its evolution from energetic pursuit to self-annihilation, from human to divine action—and this is a short poem of eight stanzas (as though the poet would suggest that what happened with such intensity can not be measured by man-devised clock-time), a poem in which mystery is presented with the greatest clarity and simplicity (as though he felt that his experience, which may be given only to the elect, has nevertheless a limpid quality that even a child could understand).

For, unlike such a German mystic as Jacob Böhme, who resorts to new coinages in the attempt to express the inexpressible, adding the mystery of words to the mysterious experience, our poet, following the sober Latin tradition of all religious writing in Romance languages, is content with the stock of words already given by the language and, even here, limits himself to a restricted number. At the same time, however, he multiplies, by repetition, variation and syntactical disposition, the density of the web of semantic interrelations, resuscitating the memories (memories of the soul and of the flesh) that are latent in popular terms. Thus, although the poem contains only familiar Spanish words which can be understood by the Spaniards of today as well as they were in the sixteenth century (perhaps with the exception of the Gallicism *ventalle*, "fan"), these words have become endowed with a mystical depth which makes them appear as new words (though they *are, pace* Mr. Shapiro, the old words). And we have again a suggestion of profundity coupled with simplicity in the easy, though far from trivial musicality of our poem. This is written in the meter of the *lira,* that solemn, ode-like form which, however, becomes singable thanks to the predominance of *one* rime in each stanza—in our poem of a feminine rime by which the musicality of the Spanish verse is still more enhanced; nor do the consonants that occur in these bisyllabic rhymes, mainly evanescent spirants [-b̄- and -đ-], detract from the vocalic character of this language, but rather suggest the soft breathing of the *aire del almena.*

It could be said that, in Juan de la Cruz' mystic poetry, there is to be seen a development of Spanish Renaissance lyricism away from its learned, verbally ornate character[17]—perhaps through the influence of the sublime Biblical poetry of the *Song of Songs*, which, in turn, we find with him desensualized: the sensual world of that epithalamium has become with him a borderland between the realm of the senses and that of the soul.[18] Such a poetic blend was possible for a poet in whom the Renaissance poetic ideal of outward beauty and clarity has met with the tradition of medieval mysticism centered in inward contemplation.

But there is, perhaps, an important problem to be faced before we leave this poem: the expression of mystic experience in a manner that appeals to the sensuous realm, the presentation of mystic love in terms that could be taken as describing erotic pleasure—is this not sacrilegious? Is it not the pagan subsoil of Catholicism that comes here to the surface?[19] Many of you, while listening to my explanation, must have asked yourselves, more or less explicitly, such questions—since, in our own age, to which few religious geniuses have been given, the Saint's psychophysic or theopathic experience is not self-evident. I would say simply that the description of the mystical event in physical terms gives a graphic effect of *actuality* which might not have been achieved otherwise. Here, too, though in another

44

sense, the body serves as a necessary "alloy": that which gives concreteness to the elusive emotion. The documentary value of our poem we must accept with reverence. Here, truly, beauty is truth and truth beauty: the beauty of the mystic's description testifies to its veracity, and the evidence with which that concrete happening develops before us in time is undoubtable: we know that this event *has happened*. We may remember that the capacity of giving the evidence of the flesh and of temporal development to spiritual experience is first found with the greatest medieval poet, Dante, who, in the place of timeless allegories of the perfect Beloved, substituted the graphic image of a Beatrice who actually walks, smiles, sighs, within a poem that has a beginning, a middle and an end[20] (unlike the "Extasie" of Donne, where we were thrown back to the pre-Dantean timeless allegory). Modern lyricism, even of a worldly kind, is indebted to such religious poets as Dante and Juan de la Cruz for the evidence (evidence of the flesh and evidence of time) which they have given forever to the description of inner feeling.

※　　※　　※

And now, for our third poetic picture of ecstasy, let us consider the scene of Isolde's *Liebestod*, at the end of Richard Wagner's "music-drama," *Tristan und Isolde.*

This choice may seem surprising at first glance,

since Wagner's text has always been considered to require association with music—that art which by definition transcends words. And it is true that here the "text" of our *explication de texte* will have to be wrenched from the context with which it was destined to be forever fused. Since however Wagner himself has included the texts of all his operas within his collected works, thus giving to understand that he believed his poetry alone would stand examination, we are justified in analyzing it critically. And perhaps it is with just such a poet, whose texts we ordinarily hear mixed with, or drowned out by, an intoxicating music, that a sober philological interpretation of the words might be considered most necessary.[21]

The scene is a high cliff in Brittany overlooking the ocean, where we see Isolde by the dead body of Tristan, whom she has found too late. In her monologue which is addressed to Marke, Brangäne and Kurwenal, and which will be followed by her transfiguration and death, there occur variations of the words of the love-scene from the second act: indeed the monologue is sung to the same air, to that melodious *Liebestod*-motif, orgiastically developed by the instruments, which in the score is the counterpart to the disharmoniously grating monody of the *Sehnsuchtsmotiv:*

Mild und leise
wie er lächelt,
wie das Auge
hold er öffnet:
seht ihr, Freunde,   5
säh't ihr's nicht?
Immer lichter
wie er leuchtet,
wie er minnig
immer mächt'ger   10
Stern-umstrahlet
hoch sich hebt:
seht ihr, Freunde,
säh't ihr's nicht?
Wie das Herz ihm   15
muthig schwillt,
voll und hehr
im Busen quillt;
wie den Lippen
wonnig mild   20
süsser Athem
sanft entweht:—
Freunde, seht—
fühlt und seht ihr's
    nicht?
Höre ich nur
diese Weise,
die so wunder—
voll und leise,
Wonne klagend
Alles sagend,   30

mild versöhnend
aus ihm tönend,
auf sich schwingt,
in mich dringt,
hold erhallend   35
um mich klingt?
Heller schallend,
mich unwallend,
sind es Wellen
sanfter Lüfte?   40
Sind es Wogen
wonniger Düfte?
Wie sie schwellen,
mich umrauschen,
soll ich athmen,   45
soll ich lauschen?
Soll ich schlürfen,
untertauchen,
süss in Düften
mich verhauchen?   50
In des Wonnemeeres
wogendem Schwall,
in der Duft-Wellen
tönendem Schall,
in des Welt-Athems   55
wehendem All—
ertrinken—
versinken—
unbewusst—
höchste Lust!   60

It is with the dead Tristan that the dying Isolde becomes united in an ecstasy which marks the final separation of the soul from the body. Isolde senses the transfigured state of Tristan: she feels the light that radiates from his still open eye ("immer lichter / wie er leuchtet"), the perfume of his breath still exhaled from his lips ("wie den Lippen / wonnig mild / süsser Athem / sanft entweht"), the music that emanates from his still rising and falling breast ("Höre ich nur / diese Weise / . . ."); note again the synthesis of sensations characteristic of the state of ecstasy, but this time emphasized with the programmatic insistence of an Edgar Allan Poe or a Baudelaire.[22] We must believe that in Wagner's ideology of "eroticism sanctified" the dead lover Tristan is presented, not only as alive in death, but as having become a *saint* whose body, contrary to natural processes, has acquired miraculous qualities that make it a delight to the senses. That Wagner himself realized the difficulty of this philosophy for the audience is suggested by the fact that Isolde feels compelled to call upon her companions for corroboration: "säh't ihr's nicht?" (witnesses are appealed to, just as in Donne's poem.) The somewhat turgid lines 7-24 give way to true poetry when Wagner has Isolde describe the song which she, and she alone, hears coming from Tristan's body ("Höre ich nur / diese Weise / . . .?"). The mystic ecstasy is incited (and this is a trait characteristic of Wagner) not through the eye that is bent on light,[23] but through the ear that hears a supernatural melody— through the music, joyful and painful, strong and serene at the same time, which pierces Isolde like a dart and envelops her like a cloud ("in mich dringt / . . . / um mich klingt? / . . . / mich umwallend"). Gradually, in Isolde, the faculties become blurred— so that she can no longer distinguish the lines of demarcation between the senses: ". . . sind es Wellen sanfter Lüfte? / Sind es Wogen / wonniger Düfte?" And when she must question: ". . . soll ich athmen, / soll ich lauschen? / Soll ich schlürfen / . . .?" we have also, perhaps, an indication of the gradual recession of the will—though the very fact of self-questioning shows that all reason is not yet extinct. But soon, a curious syntactical disintegration, echoing the relaxation of the will, takes place: the infinitives will detach themselves from the verb "shall I?" to appear, in the final period as semi-independent, as no longer belonging to a question imposed by the consciousness, but as free lyrical effusions—which are at the same time impersonal, suggesting the process itself, without personal agent: *ertrinken—versinken.* These infinitives, somehow released from the tutelage of *sollen* and *wollen* (that is, of the will), suggest sighs of relief and joy as the soul immerses itself in the sea of nothingness. In the sequence which begins by questioning the reality of the miracle ("Höre ich nur / diese Weise"?), which continues by questioning the identity of the miraculous phenomena ("sind es Wellen / . . . / Sind es Wogen / . . .?"), which leads then to the questions showing the gradual disintegration of the will ("soll ich . . .?"), and which ends with the gentle sighs of liberation, *ertrinken—versinken*, Wagner has found an inimitably graphic device of syntactic onomatopoea by which to render the final stages toward the ecstatic union.

But though there is here, as with Juan de la Cruz, a suggestion of "todos los sentidos suspendidos," the ecstasy which Wagner is describing differs in one most essential point. The union for which Isolde yearns is a union no longer directly with Tristan (who is lost sight of after l. 32), but with the elements into which he himself has dissolved: the emanation of perfume, breath and sound elicit from Isolde the desire for a similar dissolution (*"mich verhauchen"*) in the scented, breathing, sounding medium (note how the preposition *um* [*"um mich klingt,"* *"mich umwallend,"* *"mich umrauschen"*] suggests a circumambient medium), which is figured as a sea: "untertauchen / . . . / In des Wonnemeeres / wogendem Schwall / . . . / ertrinken— / versinken."[24] Here we have the pantheistic idea of the melting into the universe of two souls who have consumed themselves in longing for each other. In the words of Isolde—which we hear sung in a deep contralto—there is no suggestion of upward movement (two souls mounting heavenward in an apotheosis, as at the end of the *Flying Dutchman*); rather, that of sinking, ever deeper, into the sea of nothingness. Only in the soaring music of the orchestra, which Isolde's voice will finally join in her last note (the note *Lust* that suddenly rises, *pianissimo*), is there an anticipation of apotheosis and the sense of height—as though through depth the freedom of height could be won.

This sea of nothingness is not that void described by Jacopone and other mystics (including Juan de la Cruz): an emptiness created by the soul in order that it may be filled by God; it appears as a turbulent mass of waves, perfumes, breaths ("In des Wonnemeeres / wogendem Schwall, / in der Duft-Wellen / tönendem Schall, / in des Welt-Athems / wehendem All"), ruled over not by a personal God, but by the violent forces of Nature. According to Wagner's system, the world-spirit, figured here as the "world-breath" (*Welt-Athem*), is identified with the universe itself (*das All*): it is no longer the spirit of God that breathes upon the waters: rather *Deus sive natura*. This *All* of Nature, as it appears at the climax of the ecstatic vision, is the true Bridegroom of Isolde. The participles *wogendem, tönendem, we-*

51

hendem, with their onomatopoeic quality and their dactylic rhythm, add their impact to the evocation of the chaos that is infinite movement. We have seen that in our Spanish poem a poetic effect was achieved by simple, popular words and phrases; Wagner, however, in accordance with the spirit of the German language, must accumulate new word-combinations and compounds (*wogendem Schwall, Wonnemeer, Duft-Wellen,* as well as that tremendous hapax *Welt-Athem,* which swells the lungs of any German), in order to mirror linguistically the multitude of ever-new shapes. Again, whereas with Juan de la Cruz the genuine vocalic richness of Spanish was exploited as an invitation to linger on the serene feelings expressed in the words, with Wagner the consonantic quality of German is re-inforced by the introduction of the medieval device of alliteration (in des Welt-Athems / *we*hendem All —the '*a*'s with their glottal stop have a consonantic flavor), as if to render the dynamism of a swelling and pulsating universe. And this pulsating effect is further enhanced by the insistent multiplication of the reverberating rhyme-words which punctuate the lengthy period that extends from line 26 to 50—and which serve, somehow, at the same time to echo also the throbbing intensity of Isolde's own feelings— those of a freedom-seeking soul, hammering at the walls of its own individuation, beyond which may

be heard the surging of the cosmic forces that promise liberation. The dynamism of dissolution which
we find in Wagner's poem, describing the passionate
strivings of the ego to lose its identity, contrasts
strongly with the quiet control that informs the
Spanish poem, wherein the soul is allowed to remain
individualized—just as we have the contrast between union with the ungraspable forces of the universe, and union with a personal God: indeed, these
contrasts are interdependent.

We come now to the last two lines: "unbewusst—
/ höchste Lust!", where we find an epigramamtically
isolated equation (soldered by the rhyme) between
the two terms on which is built the philosophy of
Wagner (which is not that of Descartes or Kant, but
that of Schopenhauer): the highest rapture (*Lust*)
is freedom from consciousness and individuation:
Nirvana. But it is only an *expectation* of rapture that
is suggested by the final word *Lust* (which, as we
have said, rises unexpectedly above the low notes
of "ertrinken— / versinken"). In the Spanish poem
all expectations have been fulfilled when we come,
or even before we come, to the final *olvidado*—on
which the voice may only sink; but here, we must
leave the soul on the threshold of new experiences,
or paradises, timidly, hesitatingly glimpsed: "un-
endliche Werdelust" which lingers after the close of
the poem.

We may note also that this "unbewusst—/höchste Lust" is a significant variation on the passage from the love-duet of the second act: "ein-bewusst: /.../ höchste Liebes-Lust!" *Ein-bewusst* (= "uni-conscious"), said of the two lovers, is replaced by *unbewusst* (= "unconscious"), said of Isolde alone; and *höchste Liebeslust* has become simply *höchste Lust*. By this parallelism of words (reenforced by the identity of the musical motif) Wagner is obviously suggesting that for him the ecstasy of death is a consummation of the ecstasy of love: for love, as portrayed in the second act, was associated with night and death (the expression *Liebes-Tod* itself is found in this scene) and was already defined as an extinction of individuation: an extinction achieved not in the light of day, which outlines sharply the separate individualities, but in the night of love, which makes them one: "ewig einig, / ungetrennt"; "ohne Nennen, / ohne Trennen." Thus Death represents only a more radical process by which individuality is dissolved; Death is an eternal night of Love. And just as in Wagner's idea of love the craving for death is implied, so, with him, death itself has the quality of erotic ecstasy. That the love-scene and the death-scene should be set to the same voluptuous music, suggests that in the former there is stressed death-in-love, in the latter love-in-death: thus the expression *Liebestod* is ambivalent. It may

54

even have a third meaning: "death *to* love"—a farewell to love; for is not the dying Isolde freeing herself from the fetters of that murderous instinct of
sex? Perhaps the Wagner of the Wesendonk period,
who himself could not find rest from the obsession
of passion, has let Isolde, that Valkyrie of the senses,
die a vicarious death *for him?*

We have already mentioned several differences of
detail between the German and the Spanish poem:
we see now that they are diametrically opposed in
their treatment of love. Wagner would glorify
eroticism by raising it to the height of a new mysticism; Juan de la Cruz would glorify (that is, make
actual) the spiritual mystic union, by descending to
the medium of the flesh. Wagner's is a pantheistic,
pan-erotic universe; the world of Juan de la Cruz is
ruled by the love of God.

Whereas to the Church Fathers erotic love was
only a lowly reflection of love for God, to Wagner,
a Freudian before Freud, it is the erotic which is the
source of all varieties of love.[25] But it cannot be said
that the erotic pantheism of Wagner is rooted in
naïve, healthy confidence in the senses, as was true
of the Greeks, or of a Goethe or a Walt Whitman:
it is tinged with melancholy and pessimism. Wagner
is inspired by the desire to drown the burden of life
and of his individuality in love, death—and in the
music of the love-death. He would not have sung of

the blades of grass.[26] His flowers are opium-scented
fleurs du mal, in contrast to the delicate white lilies
of Juan de la Cruz and the fresh violets of Donne.

Aesthetically considered, it must be said that the
poetic form chosen by Wagner as an expression of
his philosophy is just as convincing as is that of Juan
de la Cruz (and surely the German master has con-
quered with his Dionysiac music more souls than
has any artist of any other nation). But underlying
the artistic form of Wagner's poetry (and the "un-
endliche Melodie" of his music), there is the ultimate formlessness of his philosophy. For the desire
to escape from one's individuality, whether through
love, through death, or through music—a tendency
which has led to tragic consequences in the German
history of the 19th and 20th centuries—is an essentially formless and nihilistic desire to succumb to
the chaos of the universe. But the mystic philosophy
that would preserve and purify the personality,
which should be annihilated only before the Creator, is a triumph of inward form over the chaos of
the world.

The climax of desire is represented in our two
poems by the two reflexive verbs *mich verhauchen*
and *dejéme:* it is characteristic that the first refers
to the sheer physical process of evaporation, the
second to a deliberate act willed by a moral being.

NOTES

1. Prof. Don Cameron Allen, who attracted my attention to Donne's poem, pointed out to me a similarity in décor with a poem found in Sir Philip Sidney (*The Complete Works*, ed. Feuillerat, II, 274).

2. The "pregnant banke swel'd up to rest the violets reclining head" is obviously a feature belonging to the literary "ideal landscape," a *topos* recently treated by E. R. Curtius, *Europäische Literatur und lateinisches Mittelalter* (Bern, 1948), p. 196 et seq.; the ultimate sources are such passages as Virgil, *Bucolics* III, 55-57:

> Dicite, quandoquidem *in molli consedimus herba,*
> Et nunc omnis ager, nunc omnis *parturit* arbos;
> Nunc frondent silvae; nunc formosissimus annus.

This is exactly the *décor* to be found in Donne's poem: a spot in nature, made beautiful by exuberant vegetation, inviting repose and enjoyment. In another ideal landscape of Virgil (*Buc.* II, 45 et seq.), we find eight species of flowers mentioned and with the late Roman poet Tiberianus, four (among them also the violets: "tum nemus fragrabat omne violarum spiritu"); Donne, however, mentions only the violet, probably because he wished to emphasize the climate of love, for, with the ancients, the violet is the flower symbolic of love: "tinctus viola pallor amantium" (Horace, *Odes* III, 10): "palleat omnis amans, hic est color aptus amanti" (Ovid, *Ars amatoria* I, 729). Cf. in Petrarch "S'un *pallor di viola e d'amor* tinto," "*Amorosette* e *pallide viole*" (*Concordanze delle Rime di Fr. Petrarca,* ed. McKenzie, s.v. *viola*); in Camoens "Pintando estava alí Zéfiro e Flora/As *violas da côr dos amadores*" (*Lusiads* IX, 61; cf. Richard F. Burton, "Camoens" II, 657).

3. A suggestion I owe to Professor Allen.

4. Jean Baruzi, *Saint Jean de la Croix et le problème de l'expérience mystique,* 2nd ed., Paris, 1931.

5. Dámaso Alonso, *La poesía de San Juan de la Cruz,* Madrid, 1942.

6. This observation has not been made by Dámaso Alonso, who speaks only of the "scarcity of verbs" in the first part of the poem (p. 184); according to Alonso, if I have understood him correctly, the nominal constructions predominate. I would say that, not to speak of the last stanza in which the verbs undoubtedly predominate, even in the first three stanzas the strength of the one verb *salí*, on which, according to Alonso's own analysis, all the circumstantial adverbs and parentheses hang, is rather increased: the main verb is not "absent"; on the contrary, it makes itself felt in the sustaining power it has, in the support it gives to the nominal phrases: the *salí* symbolizes the calm will-power of that soul that makes its way toward its goal, unperturbed by loneliness and night.

6a. Cf. the didactic exposition of this convention in Old Provençal passages, such as:

> Fals amador mi fan gran destorbier,
> Car son janglos, enojos, mal parlier;
> Mas ieu pero tenc *la dreita carrau*
> E vauc avan *suavet* e *a frau.*
> Qu'eu l'auzi dir en un ver reprovier:
> Per trop parlar creisson maint encombrier;
> Per qu'eu *m'en cel* a tot homen carnau.

(translated by Shepard and Chambers, *Romance Philology,* II (1948), 86: "False lovers irritate me greatly, for they are indiscreet, tiresome, evil speakers; nonetheless, I keep to the straight road and go forward gently and secretly. I have heard it said in a true saying: Many evils come from overmuch talk; wherefore I hide my secret from every mortal man"). I have italicized the Old Provençal expressions which foreshadow those of Juan de la Cruz; the lonely path of the loving soul quietly wandering toward its sure goal is already anticipated here.

6b. For this quite unclassical and un-Platonic conception of darkness cf. the masterly article of Rudolf Bultmann, "Zur Geschichte der Lichtsymbolik im Altertum" (*Philologus*, XCVII (1948), pp. 1-35), who dates the loss of the classical Greek conception of light from the downfall of the Greek Polis: whereas in classical Greece the light of day was considered not only the perfect means of orientation, but also a primary source of mental enlightenment, in later mystery religions man who, become dualistic, had lost confidence in the light of day, thought that supreme knowledge is revealed to him only by the intervention of supernal powers shining in the darkness. In gnostic texts light of day is said to be "dark light"; Plotinus recognizes in the ecstatic vision alone the "true light"; Dionysius the Areopagite speaks of the "divine darkness." The Greek temple which stands in the full light of day and of which every detail can be perceived clearly by the believer who stands before it, is contrasted by Bultmann with the dark Christian church which deprives the believer, who stands within its enclosure, of the light of day, while an artificial light, an image of divine inspiration that invades his heart, must be lit for him. The Christian mystics purposely expand the views of Dionysius on divine darkness.

7. I do not believe, for example, that in stanzas 1 and 2 we have to do with "two" nights: *noche de los sentidos, noche del entendimiento.*

8. The device of indicating the reciprocity of love by the repetition of the stem of *amare* is well-known from Dante's line: "Amor che a nullo amato amar perdona."

9. Cf. Ramon Lull's *Llibre de Amich e Amat,* where the relationship between the protagonists (Soul and God) is similarly expressed by two variations of the stem *am—* though the "marital simile" does not become equally clear, owing to the masculine gender of both nouns.

Cf. also in Juan de la Cruz' *Romance* I the similar wording that depicts the Trinity: "... tres personas y un amado/ entre todos tres había. / Y un amor en todas ellas / y un amante las hacía; / y el amante es llamado / en quien cada cual vivía...."

10. Cf. the scene in *Llibre de Amich e Amat:* "Cantaven los aucells l'alba, e despertà's l'amic, qui es l'alba; e los aucells feniren llur cant, e l'amic morí per l'amat, en l'alba" —where the prose refrain *l'alba* indicates the original situation.

11. Cf. in the *Chansón de Roland,* l. 2384 et seq.: *"Veire Paterne, ki* unkes ne mentis / Seint Lazaron de mort resurrexis / E Daniel des leons guaresis, / *Guaris* de mei l'anme de tuz perilz ... !"

12. This double meaning was made possible only by the substitution of the singular *pecho* for the "betwixt my breasts" of the *Songs of Songs.* Notice also that in the Hebrew poem it is the Bridegroom from whom the perfumes emanate; "as a bundle of myrrh, that lieth betwixt my breasts."

13. Cf. in the *Song of Songs:* "1 am my beloved's, and *his desire is toward me."*

14. Dámaso Alonso, p. 70, suggests that *almena* came to Juan de la Cruz from the *Egloga segunda* of Sebastián de Córdoba, wherein he transformed an eclogue of Garcilaso's *a lo divino:* in this poem the desperate Silvanio, who had been jilted by his Celia, visits a tower: *Allí (!) en otras noches de verano había gozado los favores de amor de su Celia, del alma,* and there, sitting *entre almena y almena,* he remembers *las noches de verano al fresco viento.* But only the two last quoted Spanish phrases are to be found in the original of Sebastián de Córdoba, the sentence beginning with *allí en otras noches* being without support in that poem: for Sebastian de Córdoba outspokenly says: *Mis ojos el lugar reconocieron, / que alguna vez miré, de allí contento, / los favores de amor que se me dieron*—in other

words, the place where former love-scenes took place is not the tower, but a place upon which the lover looked down from the tower. And, in any case, the *almena* of *En una noche escura* has nothing whatsoever to do with the *entre almena y almena* in the quite different scene described by Sebastián de Córdoba. The desire to find missing links between Garcilaso and Juan de la Cruz made the literary historian believe in a similarity of situations for which there is no evidence in the texts.

15. Cf. Crashaw's poem *In memory of the Vertuous and Learned Lady Madre de Teresa:* "Oh how oft shalt thou complaine / Of a sweet and subtile paine? / Of intollerable joyes? / Of a death in which who dyes / Loves his death, and dyes againe, / And would for ever so be slaine! / And lives and dyes, and knows not why / To live, that he still may dy." The mystic martyr who "loves his death" must not be confused with the "lover of death" Richard Wagner, of whom we shall speak later.—It must be borne in mind also that Crashaw's poem is a eulogy of Saint Teresa, not a re-enactment of her mystic experiences.

16. I assume that the mention of *alborada* in stanza 5 (contrasting with *estando ya mi casa sosegada*) is intended to prepare us for a further progress in time: for the coming of dawn (when the world will still be somewhat blurred).

17. Dámaso Alonso has contrasted the *epitheta ornantia* of Garcilaso and the epithet-less nouns of Juan de la Cruz.

18. An expression such as *ninfas de Judea* in another poem of San Juan's shows well the convergence of the two poetic traditions.

19. I believe that the Spaniards feel more than other nations the carnal part in Christ's personality, and among the three divine persons they are apt to emphasize more the second ("verbum *caro* factum"). Hence their mystic glorification of the blood—which somehow reminds them of the blood of Christ. It is an error to ascribe to them a *pagan*

cult of sensuous deities—they are Christian in that the sensuous reminds them of the descent of the deity to the flesh.
20. This difference was pointed out by E. Auerbach, *Dante als Dichter der irdischen Welt.*
21. Thomas Mann in his essay on Wagner (*Leiden und Grösse der Meister,* Berlin, 1935, p. 89 et seq.), an essay on which I shall draw heavily in the following discussion, has quoted our passage as an example of excellent craftsmanship: the German equivalent of the poetry of the *paradis artificiels* of Baudelaire and Poe.

In Mann's comparison of Wagner with other great writers of the 19th century, I miss the name of Victor Hugo, with whose *Légende des siècles* the myths invented by Wagner can well be compared—except for Wagner's procedure of limiting himself to medieval Germanic myths; in this, he is rather a companion of German "philological poets" of doubtful value, such as Felix Dahn.

22. The synaesthetic devices are also at the basis of the idea, dear to Wagner, of the *Gesamtkunstwerk* to which all arts should contribute. The latter idea is attacked by Thomas Mann as typically "bad 19th Century"—as if, he argues, quantitative addition of the different arts should produce greater effect! The fact is, however, that any Catholic mass is a *Gesamtkunstwerk* and that already the first hymns of Ambrose show a tendency in that direction (cf. my article in *Traditio* III).

23. Wagner himself wrote (Th. Mann, p. 104): "Es scheint, dass das Auge mir als Sinn der Wahrnehmung der Welt nicht genügt."

24. Th. Mann (p. 132) has pointed out a passage from the dialogue of the lovers in Friedrich Schlegel's *Lucinde,* which seems to anticipate the *Tristan*-mood, and which Wagner must have known: "O ewige Sehnsucht!—Doch endlich wird des Tages fruchtlos Sehnen, eitles Blenden sinken und erlöschen, und eine grosse Liebesnacht sich ewig fühlen."

These lines, supposedly belonging to a prose dialogue, are in fact already poetry, but Wagner has enhanced their poetic character by his syntactical onomatopoea.

Our passage showing the progression of infinitives from questions to exclamations is foreshadowed in Act II by the lines of the love-scene: "Wie es fassen / wie sie lassen / diese Wonne! / . . . / ohne Wähnen / sanftes Sehnen, ohne Bangen / süss Verlangen / . . . ."

25. It is the same attitude toward love which Augustine has called *amabam amare,* and which he rejected as a youthful aberration, that makes up Wagner's whole concept of love: indeed the wording *amabam amare* itself appears, with a far from pejorative connotation, in the first (nonversified) draft of *Tristan und Isolde,* in the form: "Könnte ich die *Liebe* je nicht mehr *lieben* wollen?"

26. It must be granted, however, that Walt Whitman, too, has at times sacrificed on the altar of the deified Love-Death; cf. the poem *Scented Herbage of My Breast:*

> You [the leaves] make me think of death.
> Death is beautiful from you (what indeed is
>   beautiful except death and love?)
> Oh I think it is not for life I am chanting here
>   my chant of lovers.
> I think it must be for death . . .
> Death or life I am then indifferent, my soul
>   declines to prefer, (I am not sure but
>   the high soul of lovers welcomes death most).

The concurrence of dates (the poem of Whitman is written in 1860, Baudelaire's *Invitation* in 1857, and *Tristan und Isolde* in 1857) is striking.

EXPLICATION DE TEXTE
APPLIED TO VOLTAIRE

THE PROCEDURE known as *ex ungue leonem*, the technique, characteristic of the *explication de texte*, of seeking, in the linguistic details of the smallest artistic organism, the spirit and nature of a great writer (and, possibly, of his period), can be applied most easily to Voltaire because this writer is at his best in "small art" (*Kleinkunstwerk*) where the microscopic-macroscopic procedure of the critic must coincide with that of the writer himself.

I shall comment first on a short poem, the "épître" *Les Vous et les Tu*, written about 1730 when Voltaire was thirty-six years of age:

Epître XXXIII. (Les Vous et les Tu.)

Philis, qu'est devenu ce temps
Où, dans un fiacre promenée,
Sans laquais, sans ajustements,
De tes grâces seules ornée,
Contente d'un mauvais soupé
Que tu changeais en ambroisie.
Tu te livrais, dans ta folie,
A l'amant heureux et trompé
Qui t'avait consacré sa vie?

Le ciel ne te donnait alors
Pour tout rang et pour tous trésors
Que les agréments de ton âge,
Un cœur tendre, un esprit volage,
Un sein d'albâtre, et de beaux yeux.
Avec tant d'attraits précieux,
Hélas! qui n'eût été friponne?
Tu le fus, objet gracieux;
Et (que l'Amour me le pardonne!)
Tu sais que je t'en aimais mieux.

Ah, madame! que votre vie,
D'honneurs aujourd'hui si remplie,
Diffère de ces doux instants!
Ce large suisse à cheveux blancs,
Qui ment sans cesse à votre porte,
Philis, est l'image du Temps:
On dirait qu'il chasse l'escorte
Des tendres Amours et des Ris;
Sous vos magnifiques lambris
Ces enfants tremblent de paraître.
Hélas! je les ai vus jadis
Entrer chez toi par la fenêtre,
Et se jouer dans ton taudis.

Non, madame, tous ces tapis
Qu'a tissus la Savonnerie,
Ceux que les Persans ont ourdis,
Et toute votre orfèvrerie,
Et ces plats si chers que Germain
A gravés de sa main divine,
Et ces cabinets où Martin

A surpassé l'art de la Chine;
Vos vases japonais et blancs,
Toutes des fragiles merveilles;
Ces deux lustres de diamants
Qui pendent à vos deux oreilles;
Ces riches carcans, ces colliers,
Et cette pompe enchanteresse,
Ne valent pas un des baisers
Que tu donnais dans ta jeunesse.

The basic motif of the poem is the aging of a woman. Her youth consisted in giving herself "generously" to her lovers and foolishly enjoying life with them, at a time when the gifts of nature still seemed inexhaustible, while in her older age she replaces these by art and artificiality, by riches and pomp, but loses her charm (at least for one of her former lovers). This is a bitter theme: one step farther, and we would be faced by a disenchanted philosophy of life: growing old would consist, according to that melancholy view, of having to replace things primary by things secondary, directness by interposition and indirection. But Voltaire has relieved the theme of gravity and has subordinated it to the playful variation of the pronouns of address (*tu-vous*) and of the mode of address (*Philis-Madame*). We may surmise that Voltaire, setting out to write a letter to a lady he had loved in his youth and no longer sure how to address her in the salutation, started musing on the change of time and on the change of his relationship to her. And here we discover a basic trait of the so-called lyricism of the French 18th century: in such *poésie de circonstance* the poet does not reach out for the great objects, the solemn and deeply pathetic feelings of man; he preferably analyses small events, in this case his own hesitancy before writing to the lady.[1] Our "épître" is born out of that prose-letter that was to remain unwritten; it will be an unpretentious, half-prosaic poem, still betraying the perplexity of that one moment in which the idea of the poem originated; it will be an amusing composition, not an elegy. Voltaire has not Rousseau's *don des larmes.* But what it will lose in depth, it will gain in directness; the very hesitancy by which the poem is motivated will dictate its precise form. And in the poem, form itself is more important than contents. The attention of the reader will be diverted from the motif of growing old toward the linguistic mechanism of the *vous* and the *tu,* that delicate system that functions equally well in Racine ("Bajazet": *"Commencez* maintenant: c'est à vous de courir Dans le champ glorieux que j'ai su vous ouvrir / . . . Ne m'*importune* plus de tes raisons forcées: / Je vois combien tes voeux sont loin de mes pensées . . . / Rentre dans le néant dont je t'ai fait sortir") as in modern colloquial speech, according to the momentary change from a greater to a lesser degree of

67

formality. The stylistic distinction between the two pronouns is a French linguistic convention; now conventions are artificial, arbitrary, the products of society and civilization—and we know how little philosophical respect the age of Voltaire felt for the historically conditioned: all traditional forms, whether of mores or of the art of conversation, were suspect to a *philosophe*—who rejoiced whenever he was able to attract his reader into that whirlpool of arbitrariness and relativity which he felt life to be (think of *Candide!*). On an infinitesimal scale, Voltaire has done just this in our poem: the reader is disorientated by the confusion of a *thou*-relationship and a *you*-relationship. The same lady is addressed in the first stanza with *tu*, and in the second with *vous*,—and also *tu*, and this dizzying alternation continues in the last stanza. The poet, in his variations of tone within one sentence, seems to have made a law out of his own inconsistency; as he shifts from *tu* to *vous*, he passes easily from pleasant memories of her frivolous past to an indictment of her present setting of chilly respectability: from idealization of the healthy and amoral life of the senses he once knew with her, to a pitiless exposure of her vain, ostentatious luxury. The poet who has his feelings so well in control and knows his lady so well, will not stir our own feelings very deeply—nor was this his intention. Voltaire is being superficial and wishes to deal only with the ripples on the surface of life.

With the whimsical alternation of modes of address there is connected a whimsical alternation of cultural climates, a procedure which Voltaire, the ["pyrrhonic"] comparative historian of civilizations, must have greatly enjoyed. Just as *Philis* becomes *Madame,* so the Arcadian climate of pagan, sensuous hedonism changes to the formal *Louis Quinze* or *rococo* style, with its Gobelins, its jewelry, its lacquered cabinets and Japanese vases. But this Arcady (of course a French version of Arcadia, in which the French Philis, with the *attraits précieux,* moves) as well as Philis herself, the *objet gracieux* who frolicked therein, are described already from the point of view of her present banal magnificence; we see her *without* the lackeys she was going to acquire, *without* her present rank and treasures: the first stanza, moving backwards in time, begins by gradually stripping her of all the adornments she now has, till finally her naked Greek beauty, the beauty of a wanton Philis, emerges.[2] And just as, in the beginning, the shadow of her present background falls already on the image of her past, so conversely, when Madame appears, in the second stanza, with her powdered lackey at the door, the air is still filled with those Greek Cupids and genii of laughter from her past, who no longer dare to make their customary entrance through her window, intimidated as they are by the splendor of the *hôtel Louis XV*. The two incarnations (*Philis-Madame*) are somehow telescoped.

The mass of details with which Madame's *hôtel* is described has, however, a more serious implication than we have hitherto assumed. It is well-known that with the rococo style the human being finds himself lodged in an *intérieur* filled with things: with a multitude of small, graceful objects ("des fragiles merveilles"). The sweeping, unbroken, grandiose architectural lines of the 17th century art which has succeeded in transcending man by appealing to his sense of grandeur and immortality, are broken down, in the 18th century, into gentle curves which envelop the human body lovingly, comfortably. Such a portrait, for example, as that of Madame de Pompadour by Boucher (or by Latour) strikes one by the wealth of objects that fill her boudoir, to overflow onto her body, in a profusion of rosettes cascading down her stiff brocaded gown which continues the undulations of the cushions, the draperies, the curved cabinets. On the one hand, the objects are seen as extensions of the figure in the room—on the other, this figure becomes herself an ornament, a human *bibelot*. Such a well-filled, decorative *intérieur* must needs encroach on the inhabitant's inner life. The objects originally so lovingly protective may become tyrannical in imposing laws of their own. It is characteristic that in 18th century paintings the human face, which makes man human, tends to be eclipsed by the curve of the body which fits into the lines of the room: the features become more and more expressionless, finally blurring into vague pink lines, as in Fragonard's *La chemise enlevée,* or crystallized into a black profile as in the silhouettes. In our poem, Voltaire has assembled, as it were, the properties for just such a painting; all the ingredients are there; the woman could be painted in as these require—but she is not painted in by Voltaire since according to him she has no longer real existence.

Voltaire evidently sees these possessions as having been accumulated by Madame Philis as a refuge, to which she may retreat from ultimate questions about her being and about her relationship to others; they serve as decorative screens interposed between herself and the world. And the artificiality of these screens seems to provoke in Voltaire an almost Rousseau-like nostalgia for Nature, far, far from Civilization—a feeling which for the moment the urbane Voltaire seems to share with the Swiss *promeneur solitaire.* Even Voltaire, the enthusiastic advocate of progress in material comfort and of the value of material possessions, who was capable of being dazzled by *pompe enchanteresse,*[3] can feel for a moment the vanity of man-made elegance. The disappearance of that natural being endowed with the *attraits précieux* given by nature, the being that could be addressed by means of *tu*, must evoke melancholy regret in a civilization basically estranged from Nature. The aura of disenchanted melancholy that is woven around Watteau's paintings of the sensuous, breathes also in some of the love-poetry of the 18th century (that period of senescence, in which one seemed at times to look upon the Cupids with the eyes of the Elders watching Susanna at her bath). And if it seems that I am overstressing the dismal, tragic note in a light and graceful poem, this emphasis is deliberate—intended to show how a basic sadness has been transmuted into playfulness, into a whimsical critique which allows of no deep regrets and of no acrimonious satire. In our poem is maintained throughout one level of mood: a tempered sentiment that finds expression in gently mocking cadences. Voltaire has mastered the relativism of life with the wisdom of an early acquired maturity; the windows of his mind are open, no more to *les Amours et les Ris*, but to those eminently Gallic qualities of *l'Esprit et le Rire*.

Voltaire introduces the deep problems that concerned his period, Nature and Time, only to treat them with lightness, with playful criticism and playful melancholy (Nature is a wanton beauty with a *sein d'albâtre* and a *coeur volage;* Time is personified as a grumpy old Swiss doorkeeper with a white periwig). His *épître* is a Louis XV *bibelot,* and for French taste it will never be dated: "ce sont les toutes petites choses qui restent les plus jolies," said Sainte-Beuve. The "épître" is very French in the graceful manner in which it couples mellow human experience with a lingering suggestion of naïveté: for with the French, experience does not dry out its possessor. The Frenchman knows that a truism must always have its tail twisted.

❋   ❋   ❋

Though the poem just treated belonged to the genre of the letter, supposedly the medium of sincere and intimate communication, it is clear that Voltaire has written, as it were, behind a screen. Shall we be admitted to closer knowledge of his true self in his prose letters?

Let us next examine a private (or semi-private) letter, a note of only ten lines, which is another perfect example of an eighteenth-century *Kleinkunstwerk.* This letter attracted my attention seventeen years ago (*Romanische Stil- und Literaturstudien,* II), because of its manifold planes of feeling, and has recently been further commented upon by Professor Erich Auerbach in his book *Mimesis* (Bern, 1946). In this presentation, I shall have occasion to

73

mention a valuable suggestion of his which has led me to new conclusions.

The recipient of the letter we shall study was that perfect *grande dame,* who was a militant Protestant reformer and herself a brilliant letter-writer, Mme Susanne Necker, then forty-one years old, the happy wife of the Swiss banker and French statesman Baron Necker, and the mother of Madame de Staël. It was written by the seventy-six-year-old patriarch of Ferney on the occasion of the visit of the sculptor Pigalle (the protégé of Louis XV and Madame de Pompadour), who came to Ferney in order to model a statue of Voltaire—the statue still preserved today in the Paris *Institut,* which shows with naturalistic emphasis on anatomical detail, the sage in heroic nakedness, sitting on a tree-trunk.

A Madame Necker[4]

Ferney, 19 juin 1770

Quand les gens de mon village ont vu Pigalle déployer quelques instruments de son art: Tiens, tiens, disaient-ils, on va le disséquer; cela sera drôle. C'est ainsi, madame, vous le savez, que tout spectacle amuse les hommes; on va également aux marionnettes, au feu de la Saint-Jean, à l'Opéra-Comique, à la grand'messe, à un enterrement. Ma statue fera sourire quelques philosophes, et renfrognera les sourcils éprouvés de quelque coquin d'hypocrite ou de quelque polisson de folliculaire: vanité des vanités!

Mais tout n'est pas vanité; ma tendre reconnaissance pour mes amis et surtout pour vous, madame,
n'est pas vanité.

Mille tendres obéissances à M. Necker.

The letter opens brusquely with a jocosely macabre anecdote: the people of Ferney, mistaking the
tools of the sculptor for those of the dissector, anticipate in great good humor the imminent dissection of
the aged, though still living, Voltaire; this calmly
reported anecdote is followed by an impersonal general statement concerned with the natural human
proclivity to sensationalism; finally, the writer makes
a point of excluding from human vanity the equally
human feeling of tenderness for one's friends—and,
more specifically, of his own feelings of friendship
for Mme Necker (only in this last part do we per-
ceive, at least at first reading, a personal note). Thus
we are offered a tripartite structure: 1. the anecdote; 2. the general maxim; 3. the final tribute.

But we shall find no sharp lines of demarcation
between these divisions; with Voltaire, the three
parts merge imperceptibly, so that the whole pos-
sesses what French painters call *du fondu*. If, for
example, we seek to find where the second part begins, we shall see how Voltaire has mastered the
Horatian *suavitas* of transition, learned in the school
of Boileau and La Fontaine;[5] the opening anecdote
and the didactic interpretation are bridged by the
phrase: "C'est ainsi, Madame, vous le savez . . ."—

with its *ainsi* that looks both before and after. But we should also note the interpolation "vous le savez," whereby Mme Necker is made to share more personally in the (impersonal) deduction Voltaire will offer. Thus the personal and the didactic are blended; a common ground of experience is established between the correspondents; the preacher Voltaire knows well that he has nothing new to say about vanity to a woman of the world who, through her salon and her correspondence, had come to know her fellow-men, and whose diplomatic talent consisted in what one of her biographers has called *ménager tous les amours-propres*. The delicate parenthesis "as you know" makes of Madame Necker an associate in Voltaire's art of extracting wisdom from the inconsequential; the distance between them is obliterated; a general maxim has been given an urbanely personal touch.

Now the second part of our letter, which contains this maxim is, of course, not only the central panel of our tripartite structure, but the very *raison d'être* of the letter; it was in order to teach Solomonic wisdom—and in the very words of Ecclesiastes (*vanitas vanitatum*)—that this "small" work of art was intended. But Voltaire, as ever, must amuse while he teaches. How epigrammatically he summarizes the anecdote, of which he is supposedly the protagonist, in order to pass on to the general question of human vanity; the incident he narrates is deliberately presented as trifling and is reported in a quite impersonal manner (notice the pronoun without antecedent, *le*, in "on va le disséquer," so characteristic of snatches of gossip overheard, which also serves to leave Voltaire's personality in the background), reported, apparently, only for the purpose of throwing light on human nature.

But on this subject of vanity Voltaire will write no Ciceronian treatise or Montaignian essay; he will pass directly to the one general truth embodied in the age-old formula *vanitas vanitatum*—which he offers not as a ready-made formula, but as an improvisation inspired by the anecdote, to become a "winged truth" that swiftly appears to disappear again a second later. Thus Voltaire, who was tolerant of all genres except the *genre ennuyeux*, succeeds in lending grace to that most easily boring of all genres: didacticism. He is able to do this, thanks to his mental tempo, which gives acceleration to the series of ideas (or images) expressed—of which each, in turn, is allowed to flash before our eyes for only one elusive moment. He is surely aware how susceptible to boredom his age was—and how very quickly bored by didacticism. It is interesting that these two tendencies seem to go together: the medieval mind, in its timelessness, knew nothing comparable to the modern *ennui* (which Pascal was the first to describe), and was surely not unsympathetic to moral teaching. Voltaire's contemporaries, living in an age that had practically abandoned God, felt themselves too close to the abyss of nothingness to care to dwell on their condition; accordingly, Voltaire's reminder of this condition had to be brief and evanescent. Nor shall we find in our letter any new thought on man's congenital weakness—only the originality of tempo and *mise en scène*. Voltaire, himself an Old Testamentary, kingly patriarch (thoroughly un-Christian, he preferred the Jewish patriarchs to the Christian saints—for very earthly reasons: because "ils vivaient cent ans et dormaient avec leur servantes"), assumes for a moment a Solomonic attitude, to which a jest has given the cue and which is immediately afterwards abandoned.

Ancient wisdom given wings by grace; the inconsequential made noble by *esprit;* enlightenment joining forces with the rococo spirit—these are the ingredients we shall find in our letter, which I can define only in the German terms: "ein aufklärerisches Rococobillet,"

But before we turn to consider in detail Voltaire's witty handling of the Solomonic theme drawn from the opening anecdote of the letter, let us pause a moment to dwell on the concrete incident itself: Voltaire's naked (dead) body considered by the townsfolk as the object of the dissector's knife. Here the macabre implications of the actual situation do not need to be exposed to the reader by the commentator as, in the preceding poem, the inherent melancholy of the background was stressed. Here a grim reality stands bare before us. A man contemplating his own body as already dead—this is a typical theme of baroque art, according to which we must expect the same conclusion as that of Ecclesiastes: man's body must return to the dust whence it came. A typical instance of this theme is the painting of Valdés Leal (1691) in the *Hospital de la Caridad* at Seville, which shows a king and a bishop in princely attire, lying in state, their faces eaten by the putrefaction of death. The inscription reads: *Finis Gloriae Mundi*. To show earthly potentates struck down at the acme of their worldly power, revealing the state of bodily decay wrought by the great Equalizer, was a favorite device of the Baroque period, which thus transmitted the motif of the dance of Death of the waning Middle Ages to the pre-romantic eighteenth century, whose graveyard poetry, culminating in Goethe's poem on Schiller's skull, is a derivative of baroque art. The more naturalistically the latter depicted the carrion of man's flesh; the more the stench of death (and, here, the modern reader is reminded of Hemingway) hit the reader or the spectator—the more incisive the

79

lesson for vainglorious man about his congenital frailty was thought to be. As for Voltaire, he even adds to the ghastliness of the theme by suggesting that it is his own body (and it would be that of a prince of intellect) which is to be reduced soon to the state of dead flesh. As a matter of fact, we may find, in another letter to Madame Necker, dated one month earlier (and also prompted by the arrangements for his statue by Pigalle), evidence to the effect that he felt a strange, bewildered satisfaction in noticing the gradual progress of death in his still living body. "Il faudrait que j'eusse un visage; on n'en devinerait à peine la place. Mes yeux sont enfoncés de trois pouces, mes joues sont du vieux parchemin mal collé sur des os qui ne tiennent à rien. Le peu de dents que j'avais est parti. . . . On n'a jamais sculpté un pauvre homme en cet état." Similar to the baroque painter Rembrandt, who in his different self-portraits faithfully renders the various stages of the progressive disintegration of his face, up to the final portrait, which shows the complete obliteration of anything resembling a human feature, Voltaire, with the same naturalistic curiosity, is observing his own bodily decadence. He knows his mind to be still alert and youthful, and, as no painter could do, the writer in him is able to show this vital mind at work—on the very problem of bodily decay. Voltaire, dualistic like Descartes and little apt to see in the body the imprint of the mind, as did Goethe when looking upon the skull of his friend, has no fear of splitting his personality into a dead body and a living mind, of pitting the mind of Voltaire the observer against the body of Voltaire the observed. The universe in which a Voltaire lived was no longer an integrated one: he could not, like Montaigne or Pascal, accept the *humaine condition,* the congenital weakness of man, which must make him humble before his Maker. Instead, intellect and body being radically separated, as it were estranged from each other, and no transcendental reconciliation of the two principles being at hand, it is to assert his intellectual powers that he exposes the decay of his body. Voltaire in this earlier letter to Madame Necker had spoken as "an old man severed from many things and somehow from himself"[6]—but clever, alert, sharp eyes look at us out of his old face, as in Houdon's bust.

Returning to our letter, where the motivating incident itself was such as to bring home most brutally to the author the idea of imminent death, we must acknowledge the fact that he says nothing of his death or of his bodily decay (in the pronoun *le* already mentioned as indicating Voltaire's impersonal attitude, it is to be noted that the body as such does not figure). It must be said then that Voltaire asserts the supremacy of his mind, not by deliberately mas-

81

tering the problem of bodily frailty—but by elegant-
ly discarding it. Indeed, the idea of death itself is
treated as merely one among several spectacles by
which silly humanity is attracted; thus Voltaire turns
this incident, supposedly concerning himself, into
an occasion for showing his scorn of the intellectual
weakness of man in general: his sensationalism and
his vanity. It is not to humiliate himself before God,
but to lift himself above the common man that he
quotes the *vanitas vanitatum*, whose meaning he has
singularly narrowed down.

And yet he is not indignant at the prospect that
his neighbors would enjoy the spectacle of his dissection; he calmly writes of it as if he were amused
at the idea of amusement. But perhaps we should
give more credit to his wit and powers of invention
than to his noble stoicism if—as Professor Auerbach
suggests—Voltaire himself has made up the whole
macabre incident. Auerbach very reasonably argues
that the peasants of Ferney must have known as
little of dissection as of sculpture; that in any case
the fame of Pigalle would have left them in no doubt
about his profession; and that, during the ten years
of Voltaire's stay among them, they must have become used to the arrival of artists at the château of
the little town's famous man, who had already been
the subject of so many portraits and statues. Voltaire, then, would have invented the gruesome anec-

dote in order to set in motion the mechanism of his philippic against human sensationalism.

But what pleasure could he derive from this indictment, so strong that he would be willing to represent his own person in such a ghastly plight? If we examine the list he draws up of attractions that appeal indiscriminately to the eye of pleasure-seeking humanity ("on va aux marionnettes, au feu de la Saint-Jean, à l'Opéra-Comique, à la grand'messe, à un enterrement"), we immediately see that a shock of contrast comes with the coupling of the *Opéra-Comique* with the Catholic mass. Calmly, dryly, as though merely filling out a list, Voltaire has presented the High Mass as a spectacle attended by pleasure-loving crowds, drawn by the same eternal curiosity which attracts men to all amusements—and which has been denounced by Solomon. The inference to be drawn by us obviously is that the High Mass is nothing else but a vain spectacle. The trick of presenting a paradox or controversial point as something to be taken for granted, is a stock-in-trade of Encyclopedist propaganda. The political-minded philosophers of the Enlightenment knew how to capture their public by shocking them. In the same vein of ostensibly quiet enumeration admitting of no doubt the passage in *Candide* is conceived in which the history of the syphilitic disease of Pangloss is explained: this advocate of the theory that we live in the best possible world owes his disease, Voltaire suggests, to the quite normal functioning of the law of heredity:[7] he received it from his sweetheart, Paquette, the servant-maid of a baroness; Paquette inherited it from a Franciscan monk, who got it from an aged countess, who got it from a cavalry captain, who got it from a young Jesuit, who got it from a member of the crew of Christopher Columbus. . . . Within that kaleidoscopic picture of a world of immorality and insanity which is unfolded in *Candide* we are asked to accept, as an unquestionable truth, the suggestion that monks become syphilitic as easily as aristocrats or their servants, and that the homosexuality of the monks is a normal transmitter of this disease.

The daring coupling of Opéra-Comique and Catholic Mass, as well as the no less shocking kaleidoscopic enumeration of the *Candide* passage, meets the requirements of French *esprit*, which Voltaire himself defined as the faculty of making quick rapprochements: *tu as des idees combinées, tu dis esprit.* Nietzsche, himself a past master in French aphoristic thinking, has pointed out that *esprit*, that typical trait of the modern Frenchman, is not to be confused with Greek reason, which is general and timeless. *Esprit*, I would say, is a pointed and accelerated mode of reasoning, developed in France at a time when meditation of eternal verities had become obsolete, and boredom had begun to threaten our civilization.[8] The desire for acceleration could go so far that a French *abbé* was supposed to have said, when asked for his opinion of an epigram in two lines: "Il y a des longueurs." Rivarol has defined *esprit*, in terms of time-consciousness, as "cette faculté qui voit *vite*, brille et frappe. La vivacité est son essence: un trait et un éclair sont ses emblèmes." In our passage the *allegro con brio* of the rapprochement is in the service of a larger music: Encyclopedist propaganda never tired of dinning into the ears of the public: "The Church is an impostor." But here Voltaire does not attempt to *écraser l'infâme;* he uses, only, as though in passing, the elegant stiletto of *esprit*.

So far we have spoken only of the rapprochement of Comic Opera and High Mass: in the list of spectacles which we are supposed to accept as homogeneous there are five items, of which the three first (*marionnettes, feu de la Saint-Jean, Opéra-Comique*) represent undoubtedly gay, worldly amusements. Then follow the two examples of solemnity (*grand'messe, enterrement*); should we not rather have expected a sequence of three as counterbalance? Perhaps there *were* three, originally: after having gone, in his enumeration of "spectacles" from celebration of the mass to funeral obsequies, Voltaire may have thought: "People

85

could enjoy a public dissection: the dissection of my own body would probably amuse them";[9] and thus he may have been led to invent the gruesome anecdote which was finally to appear at the beginning of his letter—in order to make his diatribe seem to grow out of a concrete situation, so starkly dramatic that all preliminaries can be dispensed with, the tempo enormously accelerated, and the tone of his letter fixed from the start. And the "Ce sera drôle," which he invented for his peasants to say at his expense, will now color everything, including the church ceremonies. This assumption is, of course, pure guesswork on my part, but it is at least as valid as would be the naïve belief in the literal truth of the words of Voltaire—for whom a *supercherie littéraire* was no sin. If my modification of Auerbach's theory should be true, the introduction of the macabre theme would be only an intellectual game of Voltaire, playing in Rococo fashion with the Baroque theme of annihilation. Voltaire indeed never offers descriptions in the pure genre of the *terribile*. The horrors he so readily describes are intellectually contrived, generally in order to prove a thesis. And the reading public responds accordingly: though *Candide* contains more atrocities than any Nazi film, no one has ever read it with shudders of horror.

If Voltaire had left the reference to his own dissection at the end of his list of spectacles, we should

then have, apparently, an easy transition to the next
sentence beginning with "ma statue"—an association
being formed in his mind between two different ex-
posures of his dead anatomy. But the fact that Voltaire has deliberately removed the link must mean
that he did not wish to present directly such an association to his reader. And with this apparent link
removed, it must be admitted that there is a sharp
break between the two sentences—a break quite un-
usual in Voltaire's fluid writing with its logically im-
peccable concatenation of thoughts. It is true that,
with the opening words, his statue (with which the
whole sentence is concerned) is brought into line
with the rest of the "spectacles." But we must still
recognize a strange shift of emphasis, a change of
scene and of tone: Voltaire suddenly shifts his
attack; the attitude he is now indicting is no longer
that of rapt, thoughtless gaping, but of sharp scru-
tiny accompanied by adverse criticism: the reaction
to his own statue which he anticipates. But apart
from the question of transition, considering this
sentence on its own merits, we may still ask: why
should Voltaire single out from among the prospective spectators only the critics? Would there be no
admirers? On what grounds does he so confidently
anticipate disapproval? Finally, how does adverse
reaction to his statue illustrate *vanité des vanités*?
These questions we must try to solve by ourselves,

by recourse to our own human experience and psychological imagination, the only tools we have at our disposal when we seek to probe into an *individuum ineffabile;* and it may be that the solution we find in this manner will throw light on the question of transition, and, perhaps, on the ultimate genesis of the letter itself.

It would surely not be unnatural to surmise that Voltaire, at the period of his life when he was posing for Pigalle, may have thought to himself: "Public opinion could find that it is the apex of vanity for a philosopher so close to the grave to have his statue made." In line with this, he must then have visualized the various reactions of the different groups of adverse critics: a few, his fellow philosophers, will temper their scorn with a smile; the hypocrites and the pamphleteers will openly sneer. And that, behind Voltaire's concern for public opinion, there *was* working within him a more philosophical concern (his own judgment on himself for allowing himself to be sculptured)—this we can prove by orthodox philological evidence. In the letter to Mme Necker, written a month earlier, Voltaire raises the question: why should a philosopher be interested in leaving a likeness of his body to posterity?: "Qu'importe, après tout, à la postérité, qu'un bloc de marbre ressemble à un tel homme ou à un autre. Je me tiens très philosophe sur cette matière."

But even if we did not know of this letter, it would be inconceivable that a man of Voltaire's critical power should not include his own human vanity in the gallery of human vanities he shows us. In our letter, it is true, none of this contrition appears: *vanité des vanités* is directed only to the prospective spectators. But this attack is so sharp and so sudden (as we have said before—and without logical connection with the preceding sentence), and the tone of it so emotional, that we must see reflected therein an inner struggle which he is repressing. What we are offered then, supposedly without motivation, is a counterattack launched in order to conceal the fact that he feels himself open to attack—according to the strategic principle that the best defense is to take the offensive.

The psychoanalysts will tell us that it is repressed feelings that make man most fiercely aggressive: we will inveigh against the evil of others most vehemently when we feel ourselves not entirely free from evil, and we will eagerly seize on any excuse to seek relief from tension. Voltaire's wrath against the hypocrites is an alibi for his repressed doubts about himself.

Here the acceleration of tempo is no longer to be explained by an intellectual procedure as before; it is the result of an emotion that must have been seething underground—to break out into an explosion for which Voltaire has been careful not to prepare us. And if we read this emotional outburst as a countercharge, then we must hear Voltaire's voice saying to a hostile world: "You intellectuals, who will sneer at my statue, how dare you indict my vanity—when you are the vainest of men!" No longer is the tone of his voice that of a dispassionate, serene philosopher, as the violent epithets pile up: "quelque coquin d'hypocrite . . . quelque polisson de folliculaire. . . ." Notice the effect of all these *k*'s and *l*'s—Voltaire in naming his enemies appears to lash them with onomatopoeia. The word *folliculaire*, which Voltaire had invented a few months earlier as a term for the writers of pamphlets or leaflets (cf. *feuille > follicule*, also coined by Voltaire), is not, as the lexicographers inform us, a careless formation, but, in my opinion, a deliberate pun: an allusion to the "folly"—the vanity!—of the *folliculaires*. And the intensity behind this name-calling must already have been latent in the opening words of the sentence: *Ma statue fera sourire* must be read grimly.

It is interesting that Voltaire reserves his anger for the intellectuals; the idea that his own dissection would delight the naïve heartless peasants seems not to have upset him. The contrast between his calm acceptance of such a ghastly humiliation and his sincere indignation at the intellectuals who might hint at his betrayal of philosophical standards presents the behavior of the latter as even more vicious.[10] (Incidentally, it must be admitted that it was a clever move on the part of Voltaire to anticipate and to counter in that semi-public[11] letter to Madame Necker the prospective attacks on his vanity, some time before his statue should be unveiled.) It is immediately after this venting of spleen that there come the words *vanité des vanités;* the crescendo of rising anger is arrested by a *fermata,* and a return to the dominant. With this Voltaire has recovered his philosophic calm and can crush his enemies quietly with Solomonic scorn. Now in our discussion we have isolated this phrase at the beginning to use it as a key to the whole analysis; in the letter itself, *vanité des vanités* appears only at the end of the main body of the letter. From this position, his verdict, while directed immediately at his critics, casts its light backward toward the previous passages, just as *cela sera drôle* had been allowed to project its shadow forward: it is the final formulation of the theme of the letter. But it also serves to bring to a sudden halt the unleashed forces he had set in motion—knowing beforehand he could dominate them at any moment.

But now it is evident that we must modify our previous attempt at reconstructing the genesis of the letter. We have already suggested that the naturalistic anecdote placed at the beginning had originally served as a climax for the list of "spectacles" inviting the curiosity of the crowd. But if this list had been Voltaire's original concern, it would be difficult to understand how a preoccupation with the foolish enjoyment of amusements could lead to an indictment of envious critics. And so we may perhaps assume that at the furthermost bottom of his thoughts lay a concern with the problem of *his own vanity*, revealed explicitly in the earlier letter. That is, from a consideration of his own personal vanity, he turns to attack the jealousy of his antagonists—whose personal vanity goes beyond his own (*vanité des vanités* is a superlative: as in Hebrew). But with that ancient phrase, he is brought to consider that particular *vanitas* which Solomon had in mind: the foolish craving for excitement of the senses, which could even make it possible for his neighbors to enjoy the prospect of his dissection. According to this, then, the unity of the letter would rest on a deliberate pun of Voltaire's on the two meanings of *vanity*.

Perhaps Voltaire said to himself: "Should an old philosopher allow himself to be portrayed in the flesh? Would this not be vanity? Surely my depraved, jealous critics are vain! I can hear, now, their hypocritical remarks on my vanity when the statue will be unveiled. . . . I would like to expose

them in advance: theirs is a vanity of vanities . . .
vanitas vanitatum . . . ah, Ecclesiastes. . . . Of course,
he meant something different: the congenital vanity
of man, who is too prone to follow the lure of his
senses. And how rampant *that* is today! What a list I
could draw up of the spectacles to which my fellow-
men flock: and not only the fireworks of *feu de la
Saint-Jean*—the fireworks offered lavishly by the
Holy Roman Church, that greatest purveyor of vain
spectacles! Yes, they flock to the mass, to a burial—
no doubt my own dissection would fetch a crowd.
Vanitas the world, and *vanitas* I. . .! I am by no
means afraid of death or of the hereafter (if there be
one), but I am still not quite indifferent to what
people may say of me, in *this* world (and am I not
vain?). . . This I shall tell no one. No one. . . . But
I still have friends who understand me and can read
between the lines. . . . I think I shall write Madame
Necker a note on human vanity."[12]

And now let us rapidly study the last part of
the letter. It is marked off clearly as a new paragraph, which begins, surprisingly enough for one acquainted with Voltaire's style, with the conjunction
mais, "but." For conjunctions are rare with Voltaire:
these clumsy and unpoetic signposts to logical con-
nections are usually eschewed by Voltaire, whose
elegance of style is due, among other things, to his
ability to so order the thoughts expressed that their

93

logical connection is immediately grasped by the reader.[13] Thus the *mais* with which the last paragraph begins must have a particular *raison d'être*. It is obviously of a "spoken" quality: "But, my dear Mme Necker. . . ."

After his disquisition on vanity, which is rather meant for the whole world than for a particular correspondent, Voltaire becomes aware of having left his interlocutor, and, as it were, turns his face once more to her. And with this gesture he is saved from other, unpleasant visions of human depravation and is able to envisage one of the more rewarding aspects of life: that of genuine friendship. The "but" is then an apotropaic gesture and at the same time a spoken address to a fellow being—though this address almost immediately crystallizes into the conventionality of polite correspondence.

But, we may ask, *where* does the body of the letter end, and the final salutation begin? Voltaire has again so well fused the elements of contents and form that we can not easily find a neat line of demarcation between the two. It falls still within the didactic range of his letter that he exempts one thing from human vanity: friendship. And the praise of friendship, an attachment arising from the awareness of common ideals, was a basic motif in 18th century writing: friendship with women was indeed, among such thinkers as Lessing, Jacobi and

Schiller, valued more highly than love: to tempestuous, unsteady and always unhappy erotic passion was preferred the calmer, more lasting, more philosophical "Platonic love."[14] It was that type of "wise friendship" by which Voltaire was bound to Mme du Châtelet and Mme du Deffand, and which he probably felt, with all the gallantry we today connect only with love, for Mme Necker. We know that this lady, with her first appearance in society, found her century "stérile en amitié" and that in her salon she did her utmost to cultivate and bring to bloom such ideal relationships with *hommes de lettres,* which at times verged on love, but were not allowed to develop farther. Just how seriously this ideal was taken in the 18th century is revealed by the hypocritical homage rendered to "friendship" when Pigalle represented the royal courtesan Madame de Pompadour by an allegorical statue called *l'Amitié!* In an age when human, rational values prevail, one must needs see, or try to see, friendship as the most satisfactory relation, practically as well as metaphysically. One was not yet aware of the fact that, as the question of man's relationships with transcendental forces gives way to that of human relationships, these latter become in general more problematic and disturbing: new abysses open up also between the Platonic lovers, and there is ushered in that era of hypocritical, half-sexual sentimentalism

95

that festers in Rousseau's *Nouvelle Héloise* and in
Jacobi's *Woldemar*.

The illusion, then, of tender friendship between
the sexes was an idea too deeply rooted for us to
assume too quickly that Voltaire's reference to his
feeling for Madame Necker was merely a form.
Nevertheless, the phrase "surtout pour vous,
Madame," while serving to give a personal turn to
the general sentiment expressed, still has a ring of
cool, impersonal politeness—which is reinforced by
its position in the letter, close to the end, just before
the banal formula, "my love to your husband." Just
how much warmth did Voltaire mean to betray, in
this declaration to Mme Necker, who appears only
after the generic plural *mes amis,* as one of a group
of friends? Was Mme Necker meant to penetrate behind the curtain, to read what every woman wants
to read, to sense the *tu* behind the *vous?* Did she
perhaps weigh the repetition of the epithet "tender,"
used once for her, once for her husband (though
qualified, in the latter case, by the more ceremoni-
ous *obéissances,* in comparison with the more intimate *reconnaissance*)? Evidently, Voltaire had no
intention of writing a letter which could provoke
domestic trouble. . . . He has chosen to stay within
that hazy atmosphere of politeness that tends
toward true affection, or of affection that is diluted
with politeness: that politeness which is as much a

protection of our inner self as it is a movement toward our fellowman. In the letter, then, as we have said, the theme of vanity is opposed, at the end, by that of genuine friendship. But we can hardly say of the writer Voltaire that he has offered a reality of genuine feeling to counterbalance the vanity of the world. Here, too, masks and screens!

This letter of ten lines, written in so light a tone, flowing evenly into a graceful final cadence, we may perhaps have forced into something heavy and anguished. We have insisted on seeing volcanoes and abysses when Voltaire has presented only the smoothest of surfaces. But this, I think, was a necessary task: we must try to dig beneath this surface he has so carefully constructed, in order to glimpse the inner geology of psychical strata. In accordance with the saying, "Decet philogum pedanticum non esse, sed videri," I have chosen to appear pedantic in order to make more clear, by contrast, Voltaire's elegant lack of pedantry. What mastery there is in Voltaire's subjection of life to his elegant French style! The French language itself, with its analytic linearity and its crystallized phraseology, imposes patterns of clarity and a background of experience on any subject matter entrusted to this medium of expression (we remember that Jacob Burckhardt was wont to read his own work "Kultur der Renaissance" in a French translation); but in Voltaire's style we find, within the given patterns of French, his personal flexibility and sophisticated succinctness, the blend of emotional and controlled expression, of spoken and written language, the gliding scale of distance and intimacy.

Of course, the achievements of a perfect style are the felicitous results of our human imperfection. Pascal, the great stylist, has said that for God-like beings style would not be necessary. Voltaire, unlike Pascal, but no less great an *écrivain,* uses his style, not to bring man back to God by suasion, but to compensate for the inner solitude of the man without God and to give him at least the sense of mental triumph.[15] He did not use his style as an instrument to reveal new depths of problematic thought: with Voltaire we are propelled, in the *montgolfière* of his esprit, upward to heights at which the problematic evaporates. It seems to me that Goethe, in that sequence of forty-six characteristics chosen to circumscribe the phenomenon Voltaire (in his note to his translation of *Le Neveu de Rameau*), was too generous in including the epithet "Tiefe"; it is the words he had to borrow from French which fit Voltaire best: *Brillantes, Saillantes, Petillantes, Pikantes, Delikates, Ingenioses.* . . . Voltaire's tempo is swiftness, his dimension altitude, his law freedom from gravity. He lifts the intellect of man, not heavenward—but skyward.

NOTES

1. It was a letter of protest against an incident at the door of her hotel which seems to have actually happened.

2. In a variant she appears as a καλλίπυγος; Voltaire is not afraid to use the three-letter word banished from decent French conversation.

3. Cf. *Le Mondain* (1736): "J'aime le luxe et même la mollesse, / tous les plaisirs, les arts de toute espèce, / la propreté, le goût, les ornemens: / tout honnête homme a de tels sentimens." (v. Morize, *L'apologie du luxe au XVIIIᵉ siècle*, 1909).

4. This letter was first reproduced in Grimm's *Correspondance littéraire* IX, 88 (July 1770), where it is preceded by a short poem addressed to Mme Necker in which Voltaire acknowledges the honor bestowed on him by his admirers: their arrangements to have his statue made by "Phidias Pigal." Grimm, in his own remarks about the visit of the sculptor at Ferney, describes the noble, calm, melancholy expression of Pigalle's head of Voltaire and quotes from the artist's comments on Voltaire's health: according to Pigalle, the patriarch is healthier than all the contributors to his statue together and "fat as a monk." Voltaire protested vehemently against this description in a letter preserved by Grimm; at that time he obviously wished to be seen by his contemporaries as a "vieux et mince squelette."

5. Cf. my article on "Die Kunst des Übergangs bei La Fontaine" in *PMLA*, LIII (1938), 393 ff.

6. Paul Valéry, writing on Montesquieu's *Lettres Persanes*, and on the alertness of spirit in that senescent eighteenth century, makes a curiously melancholy remark on the presence, in so many eighteenth century works, of the figure of the eunuch: "Mais qui m'expliquera tous ces eunuques? Je ne doute pas qu'il y ait une secrète et profonde raison de la présence presque obligée de ces person-

nages cruellement séparés de bien des choses, et en quelque sorte d'eux-mêmes."

7. Has Voltaire here imitated the procedure of medieval Jewish sources (*e.g., Pirke Aboth* I, 103): "Moses derived the Torah from Sinai and handed it down to Joshua, to the Elders, to the Prophets, who handed it down to the Men of the Great Synagogue"?

8. Cf. also the definition of French *esprit* offered by Vico, *De nostri temporis studiorum ratione* (1708): "Et cum [the French] hanc mentis virtutem distracta *celeriter, apte et feliciter uniendi,* quae nobis [= by the Italians] 'ingenium' [= *ingegno*] dicitur, appell are volunt, 'spiritum' [= *esprit*] dicunt, et mentis vim, quae compositione existit, re simplicissima notant, quod subtilissimae eorum mentes non compositione, sed tenuitate cogitationum excellant" (I am quoting from the re-edition which appeared at Godesberg, Germany, 1947, p. 70).

For the history of *esprit* (*ingenio, agudeza, wit* etc.) cf. E. R. Curtius, *Europäische Literatur und lateinisches Mittelalter* (Bern, 1948), p. 296 ff.

9. It should be remembered that, at this time, dissections *were* public affairs.

10. It is they, indeed, who bring sculpture, the art of dissection, back to dissection *tout court:* it is they who are the gloating dissectors of Voltaire.

11. "Semi-public"—in fact, Grimm (*l.c.,* p. 45) made immediate use of Voltaire's letter to Mme Necker of May 21, 1770 (mentioned above) for his private correspondence— which, it is true, was not published at the time.

12. The monologue I am imagining must necessarily be presented to the reader in the sequence of time made necessary by our human language, but in reality the thoughts of Voltaire listed one after the other may have come to him all at once, in one cluster, "Le temps ne fait rien à l'affaire."

13. Cf. the sentences from the letter previously cited

in which he describes pejoratively his physical appearance: "Il faudrait que j'eusse un visage: on n'en devinerait à peine la place." The *mais* between the two must be supplied by the reader.

14. Voltaire had written as early as 1729 in the *Epître aux Mânes de M. de Genonville:* "L'amour s'est envolé sur l'aile du bel âge, / Mais jamais l'amitié ne fuit le coeur du sage."

15. Flaubert objected to the personal character of Voltaire's writings (*Correspondence* III, 322-323): "On s'extasie devant la correspondance de Voltaire. Mais il n'a jamais été capable que de *cela*, le grand homme! c'est-à-dire *d'exposer son opinion personnelle:* et tout chez lui a été cela. Aussi fut-il pitoyable au théâtre, dans la poésie pure. . . . Ce qui me semble, à moi, le plus haut dans l'Art (et le plus difficile), ce n'est ni de faire rire, ni de faire pleurer . . . mais d'agir à la façon de la nature, c'est-à-dire de *faire rêver*. Aussi les très belles oeuvres ont ce caractère. Elles sont sereines d'aspect et incompréhensibles. . . . Homère, Rabelais, Michel-Ange, Shakespeare, Goethe, m'apparaissent *impitoyables*. Cela est sans fond, infini, multiple. Par de petites ouvertures, on aperçoit des précipices; il y a du noir en bas, du vertige. Et cependant quelque chose de singulièrement doux plane sur l'ensemble! C'est l'éclat de la lumière, le sourire du soleil, et c'est calme!" But I would say that, while it is true that Voltaire expresses only *himself* in our letter, he does this in such a way as to create a serene work of art, according to Flaubert's requirements: one that "makes us dream" and allows us to look through "little openings" upon "precipices."

AMERICAN ADVERTISING EXPLAINED
AS POPULAR ART

THE PHILOLOGICAL METHOD of *explication de texte* is usually applied to works of art and works of great art. But, at all times, there has existed, side by side with great art, that everyday art which the Germans have called *Gebrauchskunst* ("applied practical art"): that art which has become a part of the daily routine and which adorns the practical and the utilitarian with beauty. At no time has this type of art played so compensatory a rôle as is the case today, in the age of machinism, of rationalization, and of the subjection of man to the impersonal necessities of social, economic, and political life. An emphasis on the beautful has penetrated all levels of fabrication, down to mucilage bottles and matchbooks, and to the packaging of goods; it has also penetrated to the forms of propaganda used to advertise these goods. And the success of such attempts at aesthetic appeal achieved by modern advertising is borne out by the many exhibits of original commercial designs which have attracted a large public. It is also true that particularly novel and clever devices of advertising find an appreciative echo among sophisticated journalists, and there exists today a whole literature devoted to the requirements of effective advertisements.[1] In such treatments, however, the emphasis is generally. placed on the psychological element and on the utilitarian efficacy of the propaganda, while little or no attention is paid to the aesthetic as such,[2] to the artistic tradition in which the particular advertisement has its place, to the satisfaction which advertising may offer of contemporary extra-commercial needs or, finally, to the historical explanation of the phenomenon of advertising, which must, somehow, be related to the American national character and cultural history.[3] Can the linguistically minded literary historian, who harbors no snobbish feelings toward this genre of applied art, give an *explication de texte* of a good sample of modern advertising, in which he would proceed from the exterior features to the "spirit of the text" (and to the spirit of the genre), just as he is accustomed to do with literary texts? Let us try the experiment.

In undertaking this study, I shall be attempting to apply my method to things American, with which my listeners will be much more familiar than I—a circumstance which, in itself, can only provide a better test of the method. It is needless to state that, in line with this method, I shall here carefully avoid the biographical or pragmatically historical ap-

103

proach: I know nothing about the genesis of the particular advertisement to be discussed, about the persons involved in the choice of the name of the particular product, or about the history of the business firm in question. I shall seek to analyze a given advertisement in the same unbiased manner as I have attempted to do in the case of a poem of St. John of the Cross or of a letter of Voltaire, believing, as I do, that this kind of art, if not comparable in greatness to the texts usually analyzed by the scholar, offers nevertheless a "text" in which we can read, as well in its words as in its literary and pictorial devices, the spirit of our time and of our nation—which are, surely, in their way, "unmittelbar zu Gott." To adopt a resentful or patronizing attitude toward our time is, obviously, the worst way to understand it.[4] Meditation is needed in the face of things modern as of things ancient. Finally, since the following study is intended as an "explication de texte," it is hardly necessary to warn the reader that the discussion will be mainly limited to one "text," to one example of one particular type of advertising; there is no intention on my part of offering a general survey of advertising trends.

In the drugstores throughout our country, the brand of oranges known as *Sunkist* was advertised some years ago by the following picture-with-text:[5] on a high mountain range, covered with snow that glistens in the bright sunshine, furrowed by vertical gullies, towering over a white village with its neat, straight rows of orange trees, there rests a huge orange-colored sun, inscribed with the word "Sunkist." In front of this vista, set squarely in the midst of the groves, is a glass of orange juice which rises to the exact height of the mountain range and whose color exactly matches that of the sun ball. Next to this gigantic glass of juice is a smaller one of the same color, and next to that, a fruit-squeezer on which lies the orange to be squeezed. In the left corner of the advertisement we read, as the only inscription:

> From the sunkist groves of California
> Fresh for you

The first feature we will observe is that in advertising its *Sunkist* oranges, the firm did not expatiate on the goodness, juiciness, flavor, *etc.*, of this particular "ready-made" type of product, but chose to trace the origin of the product back to the groves which yielded it, so that we may concentrate our attention on the natural beauty of California. From the fruit, our glance is allowed to pass to the countryside, to the soil, to Nature that grows the fruit— and only to Nature, not to the orange-growers or those who pick the fruit, not the packers who prepare its distribution, not to any human factor. It is

105

Nature that, as by a miracle, brings forth these "sun-kist" oranges, brings them "fresh for you," from California. The commercial product (those millions of oranges packed methodically in thousands of cases and transported by the railroads) is shown against the background of its natural environment— indeed, the glass of orange-juice, as we have seen, is set down right in the midst of nature. In the inscription, there is not even the verbal form "brought" which would suggest human activity: the oranges kissed by the sun are there as an accomplished fact; their transportation over miles and miles of territory is passed over in silence. The elimination of man from this pictorial representation, the concentration on productive Nature and on the miracle of the final appearance of the juice, as we have it before us in our drugstores, represents a highly poetic procedure, since, thereby, our everyday causality (the laws of supply and demand, of mass production and lowered prices) is replaced by other laws (the laws of Nature—and of the miracle); and on our routine reality there is superimposed another, dream-like, reality: the consumer may have the illusion, for a moment, of drinking nectar at the source.[6] And the public accepts willingly the hypocrisy of the artist. It is as though this manifestation of commercial self-expression were denying its essential purpose, that of selling and of profit-making; as though the business world were engrossed only in harvesting what Nature gives and in bringing her gifts to the individual enjoyer—in an Arcadian life harmonious with Nature. In the city drugstore, over whose counter this sunny picture shines, the wall opens up before us like a window on Nature.[7] Business becomes poetic because it recognizes the great grip which poetry has on this modern unpoetic world. It is true that the subtle device of eliminating man is calculated only to bring man back again into the picture; for what, the spectator must ask himself upon reflection, has made possible the miracle of transportation and of transformation, if not the skill, indeed, the magic, of modern industry? And the modest way in which the business firm hides its own tremendous activity behind anonymous Nature will impress us favorably.[8]

Now, when business becomes poetic, for whatever reasons, it must subject itself to the ancient laws of poetry, which remain unshaken by the technical developments of the modern world. We can, then, expect to find in this business art the old, time-honored poetic devices. And, indeed, is the poetically achieved evocation of the natural state of the product of human industry anything but the repetition of a device known to the ancient and the Renaissance poets? We may remember the anonymous inscription (listed in Bartlett's *Familiar Quota-*

tions (11th ed., p. 1092) discovered on an old violin: *Arbor viva, tacui; mortua, cano.* Or again—why not? —we might think of the lines in Góngora's *Soledades* in which the drowning protagonist rescues himself by means of a floating spar—which is described in terms of the original living pine tree, that once resisted the blasts of the North wind and now resists the floods:

> Del siempre en la montaña puesto pino
> al enemigo Noto
> piadoso miembro roto
> —breve tabla. . . .

Similarly, the poet who devised the *Sunkist* advertisement reminds us, when we put a dime down on the counter for a glass of orange juice, of all the sunshine that went into this refreshing drink: as if we should be able to buy for so small a sum the inexhaustible source of warmth and fecundity, the Sun. We came to the counter for reasons of practical necessity; we walk away, having seen the picture and enjoyed the juice, with an insight into the generosity of Nature and the persistence of its goodness in its smallest yields.

Recourse was had to another ancient poetic and pictorial device when our poet chose to point out a continuous line between the orange juice and Californian Nature: he wished to trace a consistent link between the Sunkist orange and the orange juice by use of a motif which shows how Nature plans and man carries out her will: this fusion of man's and Nature's activities manifests itself in the repetition of one motif which has a central part in these activities—the motif of the orange, pictorially represented by means of the unifying orange color. In all, we have the one orange-color motif repeated four times:[9] a natural orange, two glasses of orange juice, and the "sun" itself (which bears the inscription "Sunkist"); in this representation is offered the symbol of the unity, of the harmony of Nature's and man's concern with the fruit. And, here, modern advertising is returning to a medieval form. On the eleventh-century portal of the Hildesheim cathedral, in a bas-relief representing the scene of the Fall of Man, we may see four apples which traverse the sculpture in one horizontal line: one is in the mouth of the dragon in the tree, one in Eve's hand, one is figured as the apple of her breast, and one is in the hand of Adam[9a] The central motif in the medieval work of art, the apple, is, of course, the symbol of the forbidden fruit, whereas the central motif in our modern work of *Gebrauchskunst* serves the praise of the natural fruit accessible to all; again, the momentous event of Man's Fall is presented in slow motion, broken up into stages, whereas man's progress in the exploitation of Nature comes to us with an acceleration provided by the technique of the "accomplished fact." Nevertheless, the basic technique, that of the didactically repeated central motif, is the same; modern pantheism has espoused forms of art devised in the religious climate of the Middle Ages.

There may be discerned in this device a subsidiary feature which might appear incongruous with the realism supposedly required in a genre devoted to such practical ends: the "sun-orange" which figures in our picture and which borrows the *exact* shade of coloring from the fruit on which it shines, is a quite violent, surrealistic misrepresentation of reality, apparently symbolical of the powerful attraction exerted by business, which draws all things into its orbit—which puts even the sun to work. Or, perhaps, may we not have to do with the myth of an orange-sun (figured by a sun-orange), which would have the particular function of nurturing orange groves—just as there were ancient *Sondergötter*, particular gods devoted to the growing of wine, of cereals, *etc.;* just as there are Catholic saints devoted to particular industries and particular natural processes? (A black Madonna caring especially for Negro worshippers is no more startling than is the orange sun which takes its color from the thing it grows.)

As for the gross misrepresentation of size which appears in the gigantic glass of orange juice in the foreground, which is equal in height to the Californian mountain range and, despising all laws of proportion, completely overshadows the orange-squeezer, this focuses our attention on the protagonist of the scene, on that glass of juice you will order at the counter—with the same "naïve" technique of the medieval paintings, in which Christ is presented taller than his disciples and these taller than common folk (and which is reflected also in the Nuremberg tin soldiers, whose captain is twice as tall as the common soldier); the significance of a figure is translated into material size. One could, perhaps, think that the huge size of the glass in the foreground is due to a naïve application of the law of the perspective—if it were not for the presence, also in the foreground, of the smaller glass and the fruit-squeezer of normal proportions.

But why does the glass appear twice, as giant and as dwarf, when there is no difference of technical stages between them? Is the glass of normal size a concession to the realism of the beholder, an apology for the colossal glass which had to be honored and magnified as the protagonist? According to this, we should have, along with the fantastic, the criticism thereof—as in the *Don Quijote*, with its double perspective. Thus the element of naïveté would be far from absolute: the naïve and the critical attitudes being juxtaposed. And this twin presentation serves

111

also the more practical aim of attracting "consumer interest": we see first the sun, then the groves of California, then the picked fruit, then the finished product (the glass of orange-juice)—and finally, in the glass of normal size (the size of the glass to be had at the drugstore counter) we are shown the customer's own personal glass of *Sunkist* orange-juice: by this reduplication in small, the line beginning at the sun is prolonged out from the picture, in the direction of the customer—who, in taking up the glass of orange-juice, puts himself into direct contact with the California sun.[10] In the glass-that-is-the-customer's-glass there is the suggestion to the prospective customer: "*Have* a glass [of this juice]." The imperative which was carefully avoided in the text is insinuated by the picture.[11]

If we now analyze our own analysis, we see that the first general impression was that of a tribute to the fertility of Nature; after reflection, we are made aware of the necessary intervention of man himself (not only the enterprise of the business firm but also the participation of the consumer). We are left, then, with the realization that the advertiser has fooled neither us nor himself as to the real purpose of his propaganda. That glass of orange juice as tall as the mountains of California is a clear testimonial to the businessman's subjective estimation of the comparative importance of business interests. Indeed, when we review the violence done to Nature in our picture (displacement of proportions, surrealistic use of a motif, change of the natural color of objects), we see how, in a very artistic manner, this procedure has served to illustrate, in a spirit, ultimately, of candid self-criticism, the very nature of business which, while associating itself with Nature, subordinates her to its purpose—and to ours. Our picture has used all the attractions of living Nature in order to advertise her commercialized form.

Before concluding the analysis of the pictorial elements of our advertisement, we must note the failure to present graphically the metaphor indicated by the trademark: we do not see the oranges being kissed by the sun. No trace of solar activity is suggested— even in the traditional, schematic form of rays. For this sun is no living entity, it is an emblem, an ideogram created by the advertisers to bear their label. Emblematic poetry uses stereotyped symbols; just as in sixteenth- and seventeenth-century imagery, the arrow of Cupid or the scythe of Death represented ready-made ingredients, the modern industrial labels are (or at least anticipate being) permanent: the *Sunkist* business firm is more interested in propagating its label than in re-enacting the original metaphor. (We are far from the atmosphere of the Greek world where personal gods embrace and beget.) On the other hand, we do not find in the caption of

113

our advertisement the label as such, only a reference to *sunkist groves*. In this way, the reader is cleverly led to retrace the origin of the label. Many years ago the label *Sunkist* had been coined and it had become generally accepted, its pristine freshness lost. With the reference to *sunkist groves* (notice that *sunkist* is not capitalized!) it is as though we were presented with the original situation that inspired the name, with the "pre-proper-name state" or etymology of the trade-mark.

Now, if we consider the phrase "sunkist groves" from a philological point of view, it is to be noted that this was intended as a poetic expression:[12] it is to be doubted whether millions of Americans have ever read or heard the word "sun-kissed"—except as the denomination of a brand of oranges. At the same time, however, it does not have the flavor of distinguished poetry; the expression "sun-kissed" itself is rather stalely poetic (the only attestation, according to the NED is from a certain E. Brannan: 1873),[12a] and the particular form "-kist" is, in addition, a sentimental pastiche of Shakespearian style.[13] It is very interesting to note, however, that this would-be poetic spelling is also reminiscent of the tendency illustrated, for example, by the use of *nite* for *night,* or *u* for *you* (*Uneeda Biscuit*), which is to be found only in arrantly commercial language (and which is due, I have been told, to an economical desire to

114

save space[13a]; for myself, however, I am inclined to believe that it is inspired by the more positive desire to create an energetic, streamlined impression of efficiency).[14] We have, that is, to do with a hybrid form, suggestive of two mutually exclusive stylistic environments. And something of this same duality obtains with the compound form consisting of "ablative" + participle: unlike so many compounds, this particular type (*God-given, heaven-blest, man-made, wind-tossed, rain-swept, etc.*) was originally highly literary, and even today it is excluded from colloquial speech. When first introduced into advertising, it represented a literary effort on the part of the writer—though this may no longer be true of all advertising writers, just as it is probably not true of most of their readers, who perhaps are acquainted only with the commercial flavor of the type *oven-baked beans, etc.*[15] As for the particular expression *sunkist*, we are probably justified in assuming a "poetic" intention on the part of the creator of the coinage because of the poetic nature of the concept involved ("kissed by the sun"); at the same time, however, he must have been conscious of its commercial by-flavor; he has been able to play on two chessboards, to appeal to two types of consumers: those who admire a brisk, efficient businesslike style, and those who think that "the sun of Homer, it still shineth on us." Thus our hybrid word,

115

which is without roots in normal speech, is doomed to a homeless existence: *sunkist* is possible only in that No Man's Land where the prosaic is shunned—but the poetic is taken not quite seriously.[16]

And this last fact explains, perhaps, why it can be that businessmen should be so eager to coin, as a technical, commercial term, such a word as *sunkist*, which appeals to poetic imagination in a manner and to a degree quite at variance with their own and their public's speech, and in utter contradiction to what we are supposed to accept as the essential characteristic of business. Psychologists would answer with the concept of "affective appeal," the tendency by which feelings that are aroused by one stimulus will spread and attach themselves to other stimuli (Burtt, p. 437).[17] But I fear that the psychologists of advertising oversimplify the psychology of the advertiser—who is not only a businessman but a human being: one who is endowed with all the normal potentialities of emotion and who finds expression of these in the exercise of his profession. In his private life, in his social relations, he has been taught to minimize or even to ridicule the poetic apperception of life; the idea of whiling away his leisure time by composing sonnet sequences, as is quite common with his counterpart in South America, would be almost unthinkable to him. But his copywriter feels free to indulge in that poetic fancy

116

from which his superior, the business executive, ordinarily shies away (let us not forget that many a copywriter is a thwarted poet whose college dreams have not quite come true). And why does the advertiser, whose mouthpiece is the copywriter, allow himself to be presented before the public as a poet *malgré lui?* Surely it is because he feels himself protected, he feels the fanciful words of the advertisement protected, by invisible "quotation marks" which can ward off the possible ridicule of the public and which exculpate him, in his own eyes, for his daring.

By "quotation marks" I mean to characterize an attitude toward language which is shared by the speaker and his public, and according to which he may use words with the implication: "I have good reasons for saying this—but don't pin me down!" The public, for its part, reacts accordingly: there is on both sides a tacit understanding of the rules of the game (a game which also involves the necessary embellishment by the seller of his products and a corresponding attitude of sales-resistance on the part of the prospect). Thus the word *sunkist* comes to us with its range calculated and delimited, with its impact of reality reduced; this word is noncommittal of reality; it transports the listener into a world of Arcadian beauty, but with no insistence that this world really exists. Of course, the beautiful groves

117

of California which produce excellent oranges do exist, but a world in which they may really be called "sunkist" does not. And everyone knows that, while the advertised goods may be quite first-rate, the better world which the advertiser evokes is a never-never land.[18] Nonetheless, the idealizations of advertising are not wasted upon the listener: though he cannot take up forthwith his dwelling in the paradisiac world filled with fragrant groves where golden fruit slowly ripen under the caress of the sun,[19] his imagination has made the detour through this *word-paradise* and carries back the poetic flavor which will season the physical enjoyment of the orange juice he will drink for breakfast the next morning. Here, in an unexpected corner of our technologically organized age, and in the service of the most highly rationalized interests, poetry has developed its most miraculous quality: that of establishing a realm of pure, gratuitous, disinterested beauty, which has existence only in the imagination. And the poetic achievement is presented to the public with all sincerity—and with all cautiousness: with overtones of irony which preclude any too-serious commitment.

If we ask ourselves with which historical literary climate we should associate this playful language of advertisement, which is satisfied with feigning gratuitously an ideal *word-world* in empty space, the

118

kinship with certain baroque or *précieux* ways of speech becomes evident: "sunkist" for "oranges" belongs to a poetic "as-if" speech, no different essentially from "conseiller des grâces" for "miroir."

Préciosité and the parallel baroque styles of euphuism, *Schwulst, marinismo,* and *gongorismo* (it was not unadvisedly that we quoted above a passage from Góngora) have their cultural roots in a polar tension between life as it is and life as it should be: reality appears on the one hand with all the attractions of beautiful sensuousness and, on the other, beclouded by our consciousness of the futility of these attractions, by the feeling of *desengaño*—a feeling which prevailed even in France, where only the most "reasonable" variant of the baroque existed. One knows quite well that the mirror cannot always counsel graceful behavior, but one lends it this rôle in order to create an illusion absolutely unwarranted by reality. The *précieuse* dwells in that borderland of poetry which could "perhaps" be true, but, as she knows, is not true—this is an example of the same mild form of wishful thinking which is at the bottom of American advertising. The American public, exposed at every moment to the impact of advertising propaganda, easily applies its grain of salt; it does not condemn outright the excesses of *préciosité,* as did Molière's Gorgibus; it can afford to let itself be seduced to

119

a certain point, for it is fully aware of the matter-of-fact reality of the product advertised. Thus an attitude of *desengaño* would seem to be present here, too; does this represent a general disillusionment, due to particular unfortunate experiences in American history: to the disenchantment of pioneers who had left the Old World in search of a better one—or who, already in this country, had turned to the West in search of gold—and have often seen their hopes frustrated? In view of the ingrained optimism which still today enables the American to meet each calamity with his hopes of a better deal just around the corner,[20] this hypothesis can hardly endure. Nor can we assume, in the case of the situation of advertising, any actual distrust of the merits of any particular product; there is, undoubtedly, in America an attitude of confidence (supported, it is true, by a whole framework of supervisory regulations) in the factual truthfulness of the claims made by manufacturers.[21] I should say that, in the skeptical, or half-skeptical attitude of the American public[22] in regard to advertising, we may see that basic mistrust of language itself which is one of the most genuine features of the Anglo-Saxon character,[23] as opposed to the trust in words by which the Romance peoples are animated—those *Wortmenschen*, as Schuchardt has called them, whose esthetics Benedetto Croce has formulated in the postulate: "Quello che non è espresso non esiste!" For the Anglo-Saxon, on the contrary, reality remains ultimately inexpressible. Such a people will, obviously, have a mistrust of poetry because of its too easy, too felicitous finds which cannot be made to square with the complexity of reality. Now since, in the game continually going on between the advertiser and the public, the customer is expected to take the rôle of skeptic, it is possible for poetry to be given full play; the advertiser does not ask that his words be taken completely at face value, and he must not be held to literal account for the truth of every syllable. Thus the poetry of advertisement can be truly enjoyed because it makes none of the solemn claims of literary poetry. It is precisely because Americans know reality so well, because they ask to face it, and do not like to be hoodwinked, because they are not easily made victims of metaphysical word-clouds as are the Germans, or of word-fulgurations, as are the French, that they can indulge in the *acte gratuit* of the human word in its poetical nowhereness. So fully aware is the advertiser of this discounting attitude on the part of his public that, not infrequently, he anticipates the forthcoming skepticism by the feint of self-indictment—as when Macy's apologizes prettily for its many entrances, but insists, for the reassurance of harassed husbands shopping for their wives, that not *all* subway exits lead to their store.

And, in a more pedantic, statistical vein, the well-known claim of "99^{44}/$_{100}$%" of purity uses a screen of scrupulous precision and self-criticism to advance the claim of what is, after all, an extraordinary degree of near-perfection.

Every work of art is addressed to a public, whether outspokenly or implicitly. A painting on the wall, for example, is an invitation to the beholder to engage in a relationship with it; there are always involved in the painting $n + 1$ elements, with n elements included from the beginning in the work of art itself; and $n + 1$ remains the formula even when there are several beholders. In the case of three persons, for example, the relationships between them and the picture of n elements would be $n + 1^a$, $n + 1^b$, $n + 1^c$ respectively—and in the case of x persons $n + 1^x$. Now, we have seen how, in the case of our advertising picture, there has been established, by means of that second glass of normal proportions, a relationship between the groves of California and the ultimate individual consumer. At the same time, this personal relationship is underscored (in a manner unknown to other works of art) by the phrase "fresh *for you*," which every customer must understand as a personal address to himself (incidentally these three words of personal address are printed in script). In this *you* we have, obviously, a device which is not peculiar to the picture in question but is highly representative of the genre itself, and is a quite common feature to be found in every page of the daily newspaper.[24] If we would ask ourselves what is involved in the use of this advertising "you," we must first inquire, superfluous and far-fetched as the procedure may seem, into the meaning of this second personal pronoun, according to the philosophy of grammar. "You" is a startling word: it calls up the dormant ego in every human being:[25] "you" is in fact nothing but the ego seen by another; it addresses itself to our feeling that we are a unified person recognizable from the outside; it also suggests someone outside of us who is able to say "you" and who feels akin to "us" as a fellow man.[26] Now, in English, the pronoun "you" enjoys an ambiguity to a degree unknown in the main European languages, which are characterized by greater inflection; it is equally applicable to a singular or a plural audience, and, in advertising, this double reference is fully exploited: the advertiser, while preparing his copy for the general public, thinks the "you" as an "all of you"—but intends it to be interpreted as a "you personally," applicable to the individual A, B, or C. In the case of our advertisement A translates the algebraic X of the "you" as "fresh for *me* has the orange been brought here from California"; and B and C do the same. Though he is only one of millions, every single individual is individually addressed and flattered.[27]

It is also true that he has come to accept this flattery as no more than his due. Of all the peoples among whom I have lived, the Americans seem to me most jealously insistent on the right of being addressed as individuals. It is an interesting paradox that the same civilization that has perfected standardization to such a degree is also characterized by this intense need for the recognition of one's personal existence. And this need, which is most acutely in evidence when individuals deal with each other (the relationship between teacher and pupil in America, for example, must impress any European) can, evidently, not be ignored even when both parties are anonymous. The concern shown in American advertising for the individual psychology, in spite of the impersonal relationship which is given with such a setup, must have deep roots in the American soul. And with this, we reach out for a historical explanation of the genesis of American advertising itself (for, so far as chronological priority and degree of development and intensity are concerned, advertising must be considered as an Americanism).

And here I would take into account to what Max Weber and Tröltsch have called "Religionssoziologie": the discipline which sees in economic and social developments ultimately the workings of the "only powerful lever of all civilization, religion" (as the Romantic philosopher Bachofen has expressed it). Thus it was possible for these scholars[28] to explain modern capitalism from the religious background of Calvinism: this religion, which preaches a God far removed from man and his earthly doings, and, in spite of the inscrutability of Providence, still insists on the sanctity of work, with the implication of its possible influence on the decisions of Providence: this has encouraged a program of work for work's sake (and of capital for capital's sake), according to which the individual must work as if God had selected his soul for salvation—in the hope that, perhaps, the resultant increase in worldly goods may be a sign of this selection. Thus the most transcendent of religions has, paradoxically enough, served to encourage the pursuit of the most secular of interests. Now, in America, as is well known, the Calvinism of the early English immigrants was overlaid by deistic teachings, which proved more congenial to the Americans than did the Genevan doctrines, because of an even greater emphasis on human values at the expense of concern with the divine, and an even more optimistic picture of the universe.

As far as the field of advertising itself is con-

125

cerned, I would say (and I do not know whether or not this point has been made before) that the "Reklame-Gesinnung," as the Germans would call it, the "advertising mentality," is not alone due to the Calvinistic-deistic business-mindedness which encourages the increase of goods for the sake of increase. In order to explain the tremendous development of advertising, which today is an industry in itself, we must take into account a second factor, itself related to religious Protestant impulses: this is the "preaching mentality" which has impressed so many observers of American life (one thinks immediately of certain observations of André Siegfried), and which is based on the conviction that every man, possessed as he is of the divine spark of reason (in this connection we may remember the words of De Tocqueville, who observed that the Americans are the most Cartesian of peoples), has only to be taught what is the good in order to accept it and to pursue it to the ever-increasing perfection of his nature. There is no doubt that, to a great extent, present-day advertising has taken over the rôle of the teacher of morals who, by an appeal to their reason, points out the good to his pupils, confident, like Socrates, that man needs only to be shown the good in order to do it—though, given the weakness of human nature, he must constantly be reminded of his real advantage, lest he slip back into apathy;

the advertiser, like the preacher, must "create the demand" for the better. This belief in the teachability of man and in his readiness, if duly and regularly aroused, to improve his condition (here, of course, his material condition) is everywhere evident in advertising: "You can have what you want if you save for it"[29] and "Do not look back. Past is past. You are over the dam. Look forward!" are exhortations appearing in banking advertisements; "I can resist no temptation!" are the opening words of an advertisement for a digestion aid. Not always, of course, is the didactic note so strongly in evidence, but it would not, perhaps, be wrong to see a sermon in all advertising:[30] the advertiser is one who preaches the material good with confidence in the ever-possible increase of material welfare and in the ever-possible self-perfectibility of man in his rational pursuit thereof. And, true to Protestant sectarian tradition, every advertiser preaches a gospel of his own. Voltaire has said: "Tout protestant est un pape, une bible à la main." Similarly, every advertiser points you to his product as the only way to salvation.

And, in his preaching, the advertiser must always envisage the individual listener, just as the Protestant pastor seeks to press his truths home to each individual member of his congregation. Indeed, in our "for you," we have a phrase which can, perhaps, be traced back directly to statements of dogma made from the pulpit. When the pastor declares that "Christ has suffered death for *you*, for the liberation of *your* soul from sin," he is presenting this divine intervention as working for each individual separately, and his "you" is interpreted by each of his listeners as "for me personally."[31] Here we have not so much an exhortation as a promise. And a comparable note of promise is present in our advertisement—which, obviously, does not belong to the didactic type noted above; here, the command to buy is present only in the sublimated form of the "second glass" inviting to drink; the emphasis is on the riches of the earth waiting to be enjoyed by man. In a secularized, laicized civilization, where human activity in pursuit of material welfare is not shunned but accepted as a blessing from God, it was easily possible for the mysticism of the pastor's "for you" to become diluted: material welfare, too, could be seen as something willed by God "for you," "for me," personally; there is only a small step from the optimistic preaching of the boundless, the paradisiac possibilities of divine goodness which man must only be ready to accept, to the optimistic preaching of the boundless, the paradisiac possibilities of earthly well-being which, likewise, man must simply allow himself to enjoy.[32]

With its insistence on the *you*, advertising is closer

to deism than to Calvinism: whereas (Calvinistic) capitalism, with its sterness and austerity, tends to ignore the consumer, bent as it is toward what Weber has called an "innerweltliche Askese," that is, toward production for production's sake, for the sake of the morality of the producer and for the glory of God ("Work in order to acquire riches for God!" as Richard Baxter said), advertising, the by-product of capitalism, takes into account the consumer's rights: his rights to happiness; it is "for him," for his enjoyment of earthly pleasure, that the effort of production has been made. Advertising appeals to the eudaemonism of the consumer.[33]

Professor Alexander Rüstow, in a witty article on "Der moderne Pflicht- und Arbeitsmensch" (*Revue de la faculté des sciences économiques,* Istanbul, V, 1) characterizes the mentality of the modern capitalist by ascribing to him the implicit attitude: "To produce and to sell belong to the elect, to buy and to consume, to the damned" (he also brings out the fact that the capitalist is unable to enjoy the fruits of his own labor, and compares him to the cormorant which is used by the Chinese fishermen to catch fish, the bird being prevented from swallowing them by means of an iron band around its throat). Advertising, on the other hand, seems to scream from all the billboards and posters: "To the buyer and consumer belongs the paradise!" This eudaemonistic deism with which advertising is informed is the same philosophy underlying the faith of Adam Smith, who believed that, by the "invisible hand" of Providence, the private egotisms of all human individuals are welded together into the common good. While, in the offices and factories, the "Pflicht- und Arbeitsmensch" may fulfill his relentlessly austere duties, in the shops and on the streets, advertising proclaims the rights of man to the "pursuit of happiness." It is this basic right of the American which is pictorially emblazoned in the many pictures, lining the highways and byways, of man enjoying the goods of life. American advertising thus becomes one of the greatest forces working to perpetuate a national ideal: in their own way the pictures of happy family life or of private enjoyment have a conservative function comparable to that of the statues in the old Greek Polis; though the American images are not embodiments of gods and heroes, they preach an exemplary well-being as an ideal accessible to every man in the American community.

While I do not claim that, in "From the sunkist groves of California Fresh for you," which contains the impersonal-personal "you" of the preacher, the religious implications are still present to the mind of the public (or were present to that of the advertiser), there is nevertheless to be found in the sentence, it seems to me, the deistic, optimistic confidence in a world-order in which Nature works for the good of the individual man and in which helpful, busy mankind joins with Nature in creating, without stint and with the modesty that comes from acting in harmony with the universal laws of Nature, all possibilities of relaxation for the fellow individual who is asked only to follow the precepts of reason by taking unto himself the gifts of Nature. We have, it is true, shown also that the utopian hopes for mankind which are suggested are somewhat toned down by a feeling of *desengaño;* but, in the interstices between paradisiac dreams and harsh reality, the gracious and gratuitous flowers of poetry, aware of their own unreality, spring up here and there, offering glimpses of an oasis in the aridity of a modern mechanized and pragmatic world. Thus our advertisement designed to promote the retail sale of oranges, offers a colorful image of quiet Nature to refresh the city dwellers in their environment of hustle and drabness.

NOTES

1. I have read in this connection, H. F. Adams, *Advertising and Its Laws* (New York, 1916), Brewster and Palmer, *Introduction to Advertising* (Chicago, New York, 1925), and H. E. Burtt, *Psychology of Advertising* (Cambridge, 1939).

2. The psychologists of advertising recognize the influence of advertising on the aesthetic taste of their public only in so far as they admit that public taste may be edu-

cated by the display of artistic objects (Burtt, p. 8); they acknowledge also (p. 50) that it is sometimes possible for the advertisement to provide for the beholder "a vicarious fulfillment of desires." I would say that it is possible to see these two facts together, and to state that advertising as such may offer a fulfillment of the *aesthetic* desires of modern humanity.

3. Such a study presupposes that type of "symbolizing" thinking which has been advocated in the introduction to my book, *Linguistics and Literary History* (Princeton Press, 1948); to see the relationship between an everyday detail which is, all too often, simply taken for granted, and a spiritual entity in itself not unknown, but only vaguely and separately conceived—this is, I believe, to take a step toward the understanding of the well-motivated, coherent, and consistent organism which our civilization is. It is not enough, in the case of American advertising, to admire or savor a new coinage, psychological trick or strategy, as this may develop in the technique in question: one must try to see the manifold cross-relationships between the detail (the advertisement) and the whole (our civilization) in order that our capacity for feeling at home in this civilization and of enjoying it will be increased. I may say that, in the matter of understanding one's civilization, the French (incidentally, the inventors of the *explication de texte*) have a great advantage over Americans, who, as it seems to me, are less given to probing into the motivation behind the products of their civilization; the French are past masters in establishing (sometimes to excess) relationships between specific aspects of their civilization (French literature or French cuisine) and this civilization itself; they are able to recognize even in the most trivial detail the expression of an implicit national profession of faith. The present writer must confess that it was by applying *explication de texte* to American advertising that he was given the first avenue (a "philological"

132

avenue) leading toward the understanding of the unwritten text of the American way of life.

4. My distinguished friend and colleague, the Spanish poet Pedro Salinas, has said (in an address to the University of Puerto Rico, entitled "Aprecio y defensa del lenguaje," printed in Puerto Rico, 1944) in regard to the language of advertising:

"La sociedad capitalista ha producido en este siglo un nuevo tipo de retórica, la retórica del anuncio. Recortes lingüísticos eficaces, matices delicados, que han hecho sus pruebas en la lengua literaria, y que se empleaban para provocar la emoción pura y desinteresada, se combinan para formar una habilísima maquinária verbal, que suscite en el lector pasiones menores, violentos deseos posesivos, relativamente fáciles de apagar sin tragedia, por tal o cual precio, en tal o cual establecimiento. En este caso el utilitarismo ha llegado a atreverse a asaltar el lenguaje, no ya en sus obras exteriores, el idioma hablado y corriente, sino en su misma ciudadela, en la lengua literaria, servidora exclusiva hasta hoy de los sentimientos puros."

I must protest against the sentiments expressed in this paragraph: it is surely not true that the literary language has always served "exclusively" the expression of pure, disinterested feelings; I would say that the prose of Cicero, the attorney, which has influenced European writing (and not oratory alone) for 1800 years, was "utilitarian," that is, was used for definite practical purposes. Thus, the use of refined literary devices in the "rhetoric of advertisement" is not necessarily reprehensible on the grounds of its purely utilitarian nature. It is precisely the purpose of this article to show that art can arise within the realm of the utilitarian.

A view somewhat similar to that of Salinas' is expressed by S. I. Hayakawa in *Etc.: A Review of General Semantics*,

III (1946), 116 et seq. According to the aim of this journal, which is to teach us how to distinguish words from facts and how to learn what the words "really" mean, Hayakawa would see in advertising (which he defines as "venal poetry"), the enemy of true poetry (which he calls "disinterested poetry"); according to him, one of the main reasons why poets in our time have become esoteric, obscure, pessimistic, "unpoetic" is that any genuine and hearty expression of common feeling is suspected of being salesman's poetry, *i.e.*, advertising. Of course, he is forced to admit that venal poetry is as old as the world; and I would add, for my part, that the esotericism of poets did not start as a counteraction to advertising; Maurice Scève and Góngora were esoteric poets, and esotericism has only become more conspicuous in the democratic age: the *sottisier* of Voltaire, the *dictionnaire des idées reçues* of Flaubert testify to the existence of the misuse of word symbols by the masses, long before advertising, as we know it, was invented. I think it only fair to replace the pejorative label "venal poetry" applied to advertising by my term *Gebrauchspoesie,* which takes into account the unquestionable fact that the masses have come to absorb the standard poetry of the ads. Great poets find probably no more difficulty in writing today than they have at any other time: the pre-emption of words for common utilitarian purposes has to be undone at all times by any great poet, who must always react against trivial poetry.

5. The genre of picture-with-text is, obviously, a development of the "cartoon"—which, itself, can be traced back to the emblem literature of the 16th and 17th centuries.

6. In radio advertising, the transposition of the utilitarian into art must necessarily tend toward the acoustic; when, in the advertisement of "Rinso," the notes of the bird bobwhite are introduced as an accompaniment to a lyric boasting of the accomplishments of the soap in question, this is

intended to provide the housewife with an ingratiating domestic song ("happy little wash-day song"), so that the drudgery of her household tasks may be lightened by an association of her work with bird life, with outdoor life, and Nature. The creators of this tune have taken into account the nostalgia for Nature which is a part of our urban civilization.

7. Unwittingly (?), the advertisers of *Sunkist* oranges have acted in agreement with the associational psychology of G. Th. Fechner, who in his *Vorschule der Aesthetik* (1878) gives as an example of such associations precisely an orange —which would suggest to him the whole of Italy: whoever finds an orange beautiful "sieht sozusagen ganz Italien mit in ihr, das Land, wohin uns von jeher eine romantische Sehnsucht zog." The advertisers have caused "the whole of California" (the "romantic" equivalent, for Americans, of Italy) to be associated with the orange.

8. It may occasionally be true that the industrial process would be painful to visualize; in such a case the procedure of advertising will consist in evoking the beauty of the natural origin without insisting on the necessary subsequent stages. I remember seeing a pictorial advertisement of "Jones' Country Sausage," in which there is shown only the diptych of the beginnings in Nature and of the final industrial product: above, there is pictured the deep green of mountain pastures in which cattle graze idyllically among the trees and flowers; below, we see the small cones of the processed meat. Hypocrisy? Yes, but the hypocrisy inherent in any poetizing of our animal instincts. After all, we wish to enjoy the meat we eat, and this enjoyment is not furthered by a realization that we are carnivorous animals.

9. We have here the principle of "repetition," so basic to all forms of propaganda, except that here it is no word, no slogan, which is repeated, but a single feature abstracted from the objects pictured; namely, their orange color.

9a. There'll always be an ad-man: this very biblical scene in its medieval presentation has been adapted to an advertisement of Countess Mara's ties: the (4) apples are replaced by (4) ties, and Eve, acting as always under the command of the serpent, is luring the reluctant Adam who has already taken one tie into acceptance of a second, and perhaps a third (a fourth being also visible in the background, guarded by the serpent in the tree). While, in the medieval sculpture the forbidden fruit was multiplied only for didactic reasons, in the modern advertisement the device of multiplication is exploited as an excuse to display a variety of wares, presented as forbidden fruit.

10. It may be noted that the invitation to drink offered by our advertisement stops short of guaranteeing either the virtue of the product or the happiness in store for the consumer.

If Philip Wylie, in his diatribe, *Generation of Vipers* (1943), p. 220, is right in indicting "90%" of commercial advertising on the grounds that it promotes a general feeling in the public that material goods can add to their personal happiness and social worth ("cars are, after all, mechanical objects, and nothing else. The rest of the qualities that are attributed to them in the ads . . . belong to *people*. Purchase and possession does not, in itself, do anything to an individual"), then our *Sunkist* advertisement, which promises no transformation of character, would belong to the unimpeached 10%

11. This technique of extension, by which you, the consumer, are drawn into the orbit of the picture, is the main feature of a certain advertisement of Campbell's Soups (highly praised by critics of advertising), in which we see, seated at an elegant table, partaking of a certain Campbell's soup, three persons: a couple and a single lady—the suggestion being that you, the (masculine) prospective customer, should join the group and retrieve the single lady from her

loneliness (and also, enjoy with her some soup of the brand in question).

It is not blasphemous, in this regard, to call to mind the magic intention underlying many religious paintings and sculptures of late Greek and Christian times, in which the imperious look of a frontally represented deity with "starry" eyes draws the beholder into its orbit (cf. P. Friedländer, *Documents of Dying Paganism*, 1945), or in which the tympana, representing peoples from all corners of the earth obeying the call of Christ, are located above the entrance of Romanic and Gothic churches so as to force the Christian believer to enter the church (cf. Richard Hamann, *Geschichte der Kunst*, 1933). Classical Greek or Renaissance art shuns such drastic devices of stepping out of the frame of the work of art—but, then, the art of advertising is not classical.

The imperative implied in the repetition of the "glass motif" has been overstressed in a recent advertisement of "Valliant California Burgundy": at the left we see a couple dining happily and drinking the Burgundy in question, while, at the right, there opens up before us the wide expanse of Burgundian landscape, out of which grows the magnified hand of the lady which holds the (also magnified) glass of Burgundy: the correspondence of the "actual" hand of the lady with the hand coming out of the Burgundian vineyards is surprisingly exact—even to the manicuring. The imperative suggestion seems to be that the hand of a real lady (outside of the picture) should meet the magnified hand of the picture which holds the glass of Burgundy. But the "avis au lecteur" is marred by the quite inorganic and rather ghastly conceit of a hand coming out of a vineyard. Moreover, in the *Sunkist* advertisement, the source of the bliss prepared by Nature for man (*i.e.*, the sun) was at the left, and the "life-sized" glass which appealed to the customer, at the right (closer to the right hand, the active hand, of

137

the customer), while in the Valliant Burgundy advertisement it is Nature which has been presented at the right—so that the appeal to the customer's right hand must be artificially engineered by the weird figure of a lady's manicured hand in the midst of Nature.

12. I do not know the exact date of the coinage of the *Sunkist* trade-mark, but I assume that it preceded the expansion of the "vitamin myth" as we have this today in America (the word *vitamin* itself was first used by Casimir Funk in 1912). Nevertheless, it is possible that the originally "poetic" term *Sunkist* may have become secondarily attracted into the orbit of that "poetry of science" which has developed from the vision of a world in which longevity and undiminished vigor will be the result of a diet of correctly balanced vitamins. Since oranges, like other citrus fruits, contain the (anti-scorbutic) vitamin C, and since the development of the (anti-rachitic) vitamin D is promoted by the sun (particularly by its ultra-violet rays), and since, too, there is a general tendency on the part of the public to associate loosely all the various vitamins, it would be in line with that poetry of science espoused by the salesman to present the oranges as actually containing the vitamins fostered by the sun: in the advertisement of another firm of orange-growers their fruit-juice is presented as "canned liquid sun." Again, we find, in one of Katherine Anne Porter's short stories, the picture of a travelling salesman of cooking utensils who praises a particular vegetable cooker for its vitamin-preserving qualities, and uses the phrase "those precious sun-lit vitamins"—as if assuming that wherever there are vitamins there the sun must be also. I cannot, of course, be sure how much this secondary flow of scientific poetry has colored, for the minds of the average person who sees the *Sunkist* advertisement, the traditional associations of the all-embracing and all-nurturing sun.

12a. For passages of Shakespeare referring to the kiss of

138

the sun cf. the article "Hamlet's 'god kissing carrion'" by John E. Hankins, *PMLA* LXIV, p. 514.

13. It is obvious that "the poetry of advertising" can never be vanguard poetry: in the period of a Frost it can never be "Frostian," but only Emersonian, Tennysonian, Swinburnian, Elizabethan; it must have a familiar ring, must reproduce the stock poetic devices which the average reader of advertising has been taught to accept as poetic— the folklore of poetry, as it were.

Miss Anna Hatcher has shown in *MLN*, LXI (1946), 442-447, "Twilight Splendor, Shoe Colors, Bolero Brilliance," that the style of advertising, in borrowing from stock poetic devices, may succeed so completely in acclimatizing these that they are henceforth ruined for poetry. Shakespeare could coin *maiden blushes,* and Keats, *maiden bloom,* but this type is apt to be eschewed in poetry today, when *Maidenform* is the trademark of a brassière.

Incidentally, advertising may set its mark not only on "poetic" patterns but also on phrases common in everyday use: for example, when I wished to conclude a scholarly article with the statement "The reader must be the judge [in this moot question]," I was warned against using a formula current in advertising ("The consumer must be the judge").

One might also mention, in this connection, the verb "to offend," which has become a euphemism for "to smell of perspiration."

13a. The eccentric spelling of trade-marks is, of course, one of the devices intended to facilitate their registration (or the copyrighting of the labels): *Sunkist* can be legally protected as "intellectual property" much more easily than would *Sun-kissed.* The spelling gives to the trade-mark that exclusive right to which the "generic use" of the words of the language can not pretend.

It could be said in general that the law on trade-marks

and copyrights is a powerful promoter of linguistic change—
and linguistic sham originality, and, with each registration,
forces upon the language a new "proper name" which, as is
the function of proper names, presents things as unique,
irrespective of their actual status in this regard. Are not
all oranges "kissed by the Sun"? Is the shampoo called "Tallulah" truly as outstanding among shampoos as Tallulah
Bankhead among actresses? The protection given by the law
to such *"ad hoc* proper names"—in which the usual process of
namegiving (first an emotion concentrated so intensely on an
object that it appears unique—then the actual word-coinage)
has been reversed (since it is taken for granted by the manu-
facturer that a proper name *must* be coined)— is the ultimate
consequence of the concept of "intellectual property," a concept, unknown to antiquity and to the Middle Ages, which
has developed as a result of modern man's decreasing consciousness of a common human heritage and of the increas-
ing insistence on the rights of the individual. The author
of that truly unique poem "to which heaven and earth have
collaborated" was satisfied with the quite generic name:
"Commedia"!

But linguistic standardization, as active in our times as
before, sets certain limits to the individualism of the trade-
marks. Not only is their proper-name character gradually
weakened as the product and its name become familiar to
the buying public, not only is their phonetic form not re-
spected (*Coca Cola*>*coke*); it may even happen that the
individual trade-mark, precisely because it has become so
familiar to the public, is used in a quite generic sense: in
spite of repeated warnings: "A camera is not a Kodak unless
it is an Eastman Kodak," that most original coinage *Kodak*,
which, because it had no connection with any word of the
language, seemed to enjoy the privileges of an *Urwort*
(comparable in this respect to *gas*), has acquired in common
speech the generic meaning of "small, portable camera";

140

and similarly *Victrola* has become the synonym of "phonograph."

14. How the idea of efficiency and easy functioning may influence the syntax of advertising ("This car parks easily," "This paint applies easily") and, subsequently (if ironically), common speech, has been shown in an article by Professor Hatcher in *MLN*, LVIII (1943), 8: "Mr. Howard amuses easy."

15. The psychologists of advertising are agreed as to the pleasant atmosphere created by the trademark *Sunkist*, but they seem to lack the linguistic categories in which to place it: Burtt (p. 373) groups *Sunkist* along with *Holeproof, Wearever,* and *Slipnot* (probably only because of the compound character of all these coinages); Brewster and Palmer (p. 124), with *Sun-Maid* (where a pun is involved—as is also the case with *Slipnot*), and with *Sealdsweet* (where we have a spelling-pronunciation—with none of the connotations of *Sunkist*).

16. There is also contained in this half-serious poetry of advertising, a consolation of a sort, an assurance for the average reader, to whose self-confidence and vanity advertisements are always addressed: truly perfect form, truly ideal beauty is crushing; it leaves the beholder breathless, humiliated; "there is nothing one can say" when looking upon the Venus of Milo or a painting of Raphael. I would paraphrase Keats: "A thing of beauty is a *grief* forever"; its seriousness and self-contained disregard for all other things of this world allow for nothing but a mystic self-absorption in the thing of beauty. Nothing could be less congenial to the American public, which prefers not to be reminded of self-annihilation and which is more active than contemplative. It is true that many advertisers resort to the reproduction of classical works of art; but by the very fact that they are used in a subordinate function, that they are "only advertisements," which the beholder is free to

accept or reject, they can be better enjoyed by the average public than when they are seen in a serious exhibit.

17. The "affective appeal" envisaged by advertising is not, of course, limited to the (semi-) artistic form given to the advertisement itself: we also find works of pure art put to the service of advertising—as when, for example, symphony programs are sponsored by commercial firms. Thus it is calculated that the pathos and tenderness aroused in us by Rodzinsky's performance of the *Eroica* will inspire us with tender feeling for the "service through science" of the U.S. Rubber Co.

And yet, we should not, I think, be too quick to deny the vein of idealism underlying the artistic programs sponsored by industrial firms. Quite aside from, and above, all their calculating and budgeting, they begin by generous giving (knowing quite well that many who listen to the *Eroica* will not buy one ounce the more of rubber goods). And this giving without immediate returns is capable of awakening a certain loyalty in the listener: I know of one young businessman who reproved his wife for turning off the radio immediately after a concert; to his mind, she should return the courtesy she had received at least to the extent of listening to the advertiser's words.

18. The world of optimism and idealism which advertising unfolds before us is reflected in its predilection for the superlative; each of the goods praised is supposedly the finest of its kind, from the tastiest bread in America to the most perfect low-priced car in America. This superlative which rules supreme, and which is not challenged by any factual comparison (since disparaging statements about goods of competitors is prohibited by law) tends to destroy the difference between the superlative and the elative: "the finest . . ." becomes equal to "a very fine . . . ," somewhat equivalent to the Italian elative *buonissimo* (not *il migliore*). The abolition of true comparison ("good"–"better"–"best")

142

is easily understandable in a world containing only "best" things.

As another variety of the advertising elative, we may mention the use of the comparative, which the *New Yorker* has recently defined as the "agency comparative" or the "comparative without comparison": an item is called "better" without any further qualification: "Better than what?" asks the *New Yorker*. (A parallel case is the absolute use in advertising of "different" [even a laxative medicament is called simply "different"], patterned on the popular usage with its slightly snobbish overtones.) Cf. E. K. Sheldon's article on "The Rise of the Incomplete Comparative" in *American Speech*, XX (1945), 161-167.

Incidentally, it is interesting that a satirical magazine such as the *New Yorker*, where the stories as well as the illustrations and cartoons are intended as a criticism of the easily beautiful and of conventional standards—the advertisements are allowed to provide, unquestioned, the illusory beauty and the snobbism typical of their genre.

19. Often, he is portrayed by the advertiser as already dwelling in (a rather bourgeois and mechanized) Dorado: if a historian of American civilization were to base himself exclusively on the representation of daily life which is offered in advertisements, he would reach the conclusion that this country is now an Arcady of material prosperity and social ease (and of questionable moral worth); but the spectator, we may be sure, is equipped with his own criteria, and subtracts automatically from the pictures of felicity and luxury which smile at him from the billboards. Nevertheless, while making this subtraction, he is able to gaze at the beauty portrayed, with disinterested enjoyment, *in abstracto*.

The tendency toward over-glamorization in advertising must constantly be counterbalanced by the "as-if" attitude, in order to avoid becoming ridiculous and ineffective. When, occasionally, one advertisement oversteps the mark, rival advertisers are quick to exploit this excess by excessively discreet understatement in regard to their own products: the sensational picture of the passionate havoc which perfume may wreak, in an advertisement circulated several years ago to publicize "Tabu," has resulted in such mock-modest claims, by other advertisers, as "We do not guarantee that this perfume will make of you a *femme fatale:* we only say it smells nice."

20. It could be said that the American's optimism is also reflected in the abundance of neologisms in advertising: by coining new words one suggests a picture of new and therefore better things to come. This tendency also reveals a special attitude toward language itself as something continuously in flux (as Mencken has repeatedly emphasized)—an attitude which shares with the first a basic "future-mindedness."

Any neologism, however, in the course of time, tends to lose its freshness once it has been accepted by the community—in which case the linguists must speak of "lexicological petrification." The advertisers themselves eventually recognize that the inevitable stage of lexicalization has set in, and are careful thereafter not to stir the ashes of the dead—for any insistence on the symbolic value once possessed by the label would be tedious to the public.

And our *Sunkist* had, obviously, to go the way of all linguistic creations: at a certain moment it stopped being a living expression to become a label used glibly and matter-of-factly by the community. That this has been recognized by the advertisers is indicated by the fact that the *Sunkist* advertisement we have been describing, and which I had seen for four summers in the same drug-store, was replaced, in 1945, by one of a quite different type, and one which did not go to the length of "explaining" (verbally or pictorially) the choice of the label. The new advertisement was of a schematic or ideographic character: it showed a frieze with an ornamental arrangement of bunches of flowers and fruits (oranges and lemons), underneath which were seen two glasses (of orange juice and lemonade, respectively) forming a cross-bar and bearing the label "Sunkist." Sun and Nature had disappeared, except for the slight and sterotyped reminder of the latter offered by the fruits.

21. The confidence of the public in the honesty of advertisers is an established fact in this country; there seems to be little or no suspicion that the advertiser is advancing false claims. In a country where moral integrity in business life is not taken for granted by principle, advertising can develop no gratuitous poetry; such an attempt would invite the question, fatal to poetry: "Are your words true or false?"

22. In no language, so far as I know, are there so many prefixes which tend to unmask false values: *pseudo-, sham-, make-believe-, makeshift-, mock-, would-be-, fake-, phony-, semi-, near-*[beer], *baloney-*[dollars], *synthetic- etc.;* it is as though the Anglo-Saxon attitude of distrust of the pretentious would find for itself a grammatically fixed pattern of expression in the language. Americans delight in their impermeability to "bunk" (as is shown by the fertility of the "buncombe" word-family).

23. It would seem that there is a difference in this regard between the two Anglo-Saxon nations themselves, if we are to believe D. W. Brogan (*The American Character*, New York, 1944), who has been struck by the American love for oratory (p. 131): "In Chambers of Commerce, at Rotary Club meetings, at college commencements, in legislatures, in Congress, speech is treated seriously, according to the skill and taste of the user. There is no fear of boss words or of eloquence, no fear of clichés, no fear of bathos. . . . The British listener, above all the English listener, is surprised and embarrassed by being asked to applaud state-

ments whose truth he has no reason to doubt, but whose expression seems to him remarkably abstract and adorned with flowers of old-fashioned rhetoric." Mr. Brogan gives himself the explanation that Americans "like slogans, like words. They like absolutes in ethics." And the English critic might have brought up the contrast between the American Constitution and the unwritten British Constitution.

On the other hand, I would suggest that there is an English brand of oratory which is slightly alien to the American—for example, the prose of Churchill, which, with its archaisms and periphrastic turns of speech, weaves poetry round the casual concrete happenings of history; by the Americans the "word" is considered less as an artistic than as a moral tool, as abstractly purposeful as the flag. But, even in the realm of absolute morals, the distrust of language is not entirely lacking with Americans; Mr. Brogan himself cannot overlook the fact that many slogans are greeted by Americans with an ironical "Oh, yeah?" or "However you slice it, it's still baloney." How else save by mistrust of the word could one explain the fact that after the exchange of wild abuse indulged in on both sides during an election campaign, Americans, once the election is over, are able to go quietly to work the next day, no attempt being made by the defeated party to start a revolution. The word in itself is not "sacred" and final to the Americans. The difference between the American and the German concepts of the word can be seen in the absence of free speech in Germany: freedom of speech involves a concept of nonfinality of speech. In America the human word is thought of only as having a provisionary value. One word can be undone, and outdone, by another.

24. This "for you" is not limited, of course, to advertising, but is a generally characteristic feature of the language of the tradesman when addressing his customer: "Shall I wrap it *for you?*" "I'll fix it *for you* by tomorrow." We may see

here the influence of the idea of service to one's fellow man, which has permeated so many of the formulae of commercial life: "May I help you?" "What can I do for you?" said by clerks in shops and offices; or "Have you been taken care of?" a question of waiters—which may be contrasted with Fr. "Madame désire?", Ital. "commandi?", Germ. "Sie wünschen?"

25. This personal susceptibility of the individual to any address which is intended generally, has been, perhaps, nowhere more effectively exploited than in the famous cartoon of James Montgomery Flagg which was used as an enlistment poster in the first World War (and was revived in the second): "Uncle Sam Needs YOU For the United States Army" is written beneath a picture of the stern-eyed old gentleman who fixes with his gaze, and singles out with an accusing finger, whoever steps within the range of the picture. (Needless to say, such a drastic method of attracting the attention of the individual is not recommended for advertising.)

The constant "you see" of the radio announcers is a characteristic insertion in an otherwise impersonal broadcast—motivated only by an initial vocative such as "Men," "Ladies." It simulates a conversation with a "you," instead of a one-sided harangue; "you see" (which is equal to a "let me explain it to you") seems intended to counteract an observation or a resistance on the part of the partner in the conversation. The *New Yorker* once remarked that this device is coming to be used as a means of introducing the most startling contentions of the advertiser, in order to make them appear as something quite evident on closer investigation.

26. Coming from an anonymous being, as does the "fresh for you" of our advertising picture, the effect is perhaps more startling than when a radio announcer (who has a human voice and may be known to us by name and voice)

147

addresses "you." Nor, as often is the case in written advertisement, has the firm in question presented itself first as "we": suddenly, an appeal is made by an undefined agency to "me personally." By the elimination of the human element at work, by the retreat behind things, by the assumption of a miracle to which is due, for example, the arrival of the oranges from California—it is as if we were told: *"Nature* has brought fresh for you . . . ," *"God* has brought fresh for you . . . "; the identity of the fruit-packing firm disappears within the greater connection of a helpful universe, mindful of each man and woman dwelling therein.

27. Compare also "I have arranged this sale with you in mind. You, Mrs. America, are the best buyer and the best-dressed woman in the world" (from an advertisement of furs); "For you, Madame, I have done the utmost to bring you more valuable things than ever. For you, Madame, I have traveled to Europe. Your taste is to us all we do, think, plan." (It is obvious that the "for you" pattern, while appealing to the vanity of the buyer, also implies self-praise of the services rendered by the merchant.)

28. Among the later exponents of this doctrine may be mentioned Herbert Schöffler, who has explained certain typical features of Anglo-Saxon civilization (such as sports, freedom of parliamentary debate, *etc.*) from the "religious-sociological" basis of English life.

29. It is to be noted that, in this example, we have to do with the "gnomic *you.*" Here, then, is still one more possibility of the English pronoun, which is equivalent, not only to French *tu* and *vous,* but also to *on*—though, even in its gnomic use, the personal overtones are not entirely lacking.

30. A particularly interesting example of the directly moralizing note is offered by a series of advertisements for Seagram's whiskies which preach the virtues of moderate drinking! It was, perhaps, shrewdly calculated by the firm

that such admonitions would do nothing to decrease the sales of their products; the result might, indeed, be to increase them, because of the tacit flattering assumption that consumers of this particular brand are persons of decorum (if not of distinction).

31. The reader may recall having heard in his youth the evangelical hymn "Whosoever will may come" with the final line: "*Whosoever* meaneth *me.*"

32. It may be noted that the first advertisements to appear regularly in American newspapers (in the middle of the nineteenth century) were those of patent medicines, with their claims of miraculous efficacy. It is highly significant that the industry of advertising had its inception in an appeal to the age-old craving to be saved by magic from the ills and shortcomings of the flesh.

33. The two tendencies, Calvinistic austerity and eudaemonistic deism, are often met side by side within the individual American—who can be at one moment the "Pflicht- und Arbeitsmensch" and at another the pagan enjoyer of earthly goods. In the features of the American man and woman there is often revealed a sternness of purpose—which is given a lie by their (Arcadian) happy smile. Historical conditions have made of the American a somewhat "relaxed pioneer": a pioneer who manages also to "take it easy."